TWO CHEERS FOR SECULARISM

TWO CHEERS FOR SECULARISM

EDITORS:

DR SIDNEY BRICHTO
*Rabbi and Senior Vice President
of the Union of Liberal and Progressive Synagogues*

THE RIGHT REVEREND RICHARD HARRIES
Bishop of Oxford

PILKINGTON PRESS

Published 1998
By Pilkington Press Ltd
Yelvertoft Manor
Northamptonshire NN6 6LF

No part of this publication may be reproduced, stored in a retrieval system, or transmitted in any form or by any means, electronic, mechanical photocopying, recording or otherwise, without the prior permission of the publisher and copyright owner.

The right of the authors to be identified as authors of this work has been asserted in accordance with the Copyright, Designs and Patents Act 1988.

ISBN 1 899044 16 7

Produced, Designed and Typeset by:
A.H. Jolly (Editorial) Ltd
Yelvertoft Manor
Northamptonshire NN6 6LF

Printed in Great Britain by
Clifford Press Ltd., Coventry

CONTENTS

Introduction
RICHARD HARRIES AND SIDNEY BRICHTO
7

– 1 –
The Rise of Secularization and the Persistence of Religion
ANTHONY RUSSELL
11

– 2 –
Judaism in a Secular World
SIDNEY BRICHTO
23

– 3 –
Why and Why Not
FREDERIC RAPHAEL
37

– 4 –
Islam and Civil Society
CROWN PRINCE HASSAN
47

– 5 –
The Media as Demon in the Post-Modernist Age of Secularism
AKBAR AHMED
55

– 6 –
Refounding the Secular State
CLIFFORD LONGLEY
71

- 7 -
New Religions and the Millennium
PETER CLARKE

79

- 8 -
Living with the Questions
Psychotherapy and the Myth of Self-Fulfilment
HOWARD COOPER

93

- 9 -
The State and Society
A Relationship Balanced to Prevent Both Hegemony and Degeneration
MOHAMMAD ABDUL JABBAR

107

- 10 -
Religion, Secularism and Women
JULIA NEUBERGER

119

- 11 -
God and Evil
KAREN ARMSTRONG

127

- 12 -
The Moral Case Against God
RICHARD HARRIES

135

- 13 -
Living Without God
JOHN MORTIMER

147

INTRODUCTION

It is often said that we live in a world that is becoming increasingly secularized. Religious believers are supposed to lament this fact and non-believers to applaud it. But suppose there are values in the secular stance that are essentially and profoundly religious? In which case, to write off the whole secular enterprise would be shallow in the extreme. In fact Dietrich Bonhoeffer, one of the most devout and passionate Christians of the 20th century, who was killed for his part in the plot to assassinate Hitler, did think that the secular movement that has developed since the 15th century should not be interpreted as anti-religious. On the contrary, it has been teaching people to live as fully responsible human beings aware of our strengths and what we can achieve as well as our weaknesses. However, from the perspective of a person with religious faith, the loss of a transcendent order giving a divine meaning and purpose to human existence cannot be contemplated without a poignant sense of loss.

So this is a book of essays by believers, half-believers and non-believers who want to affirm some essential features of secularization but who cannot give that third cheer.

During the early 1960s it was taken for granted that we, at least those of us who live in Europe, North America and other parts of the world influenced by them, live in an increasingly secular world. There then appeared some sharp critiques of the secularization hypothesis. This posed fundamental questions not only about what is meant by the word secular but, closely related to this, what criteria could possibly be used to judge it? Dr Anthony Russell in the first essay in this book brings the debate up to date and sets the scene for the other contributors.

Sidney Brichto writes from within Judaism, perhaps the most secular of all world religions in its affirmation of this world and the value of this life. Well aware of the genuine progress made by scientific, secular forces and the justifiable criticisms that can be levelled against all religions, he nevertheless suggests that religion can still be a source of wisdom to all human beings: but this depends upon the religious offering a credible witness to the values they claim to believe in.

The novelist Frederic Raphael also has a Jewish background and does not wish to deny that he is a Jew. But he is acutely aware of the unprovability of all religious claims and the historic dangers of those professing certainty. So whilst 'only a fool can fail to recognize the limitations of a secular society, based on a system of interpenetrating uncertainties' nevertheless 'only a villain can propose that there is anything better in prospect for so systematically duplicitous a creature as man.' The result is that he chooses scepticism rather than certainty.

Crown Prince Hassan argues that many features of civil society valued by secular people in the West, such as equality, participation in the political process and plurality, are in principal advocated by the Koran. Furthermore, historically Islamic societies have offered a relative tolerance through the *Millet* system. Today there are vibrant Muslim countries which are developing democratically. But this moderate Islam gets overlooked by the media.

Professor Akbar Ahmed takes up this theme, the projection of a true understanding of Islam in the face of what he sees as distortions in the modern western media. The power of the press, having taken over from the power of the pulpit, is very much an example of secularization. But as far as Islam is concerned, Professor Ahmed argues that it is not yet being used to good purpose.

Clifford Longley is also concerned about religion and the state, but an increasingly secular one. He contrasts the world which existed at Queen Elizabeth II's Coronation in 1952, whose sense of assurance was rooted in religion, with our own time. He argues that because both the monarchy and the Church of England no longer carry moral authority for so many, we need to get right away from them. We need a proper, written constitution, built on a moral consensus. This could carry some of the symbolic authority that has now drained away from the monarchy and the Church of England.

One phenomenon of the modern world which defies the notion that we are becoming more and more secular is the growth of new religious movements. At King's College, London there are dossiers on more than 500 of these. The approach of the millennium is likely to bring a good number of these to a state of fever. This has certainly happened in the past at key dates in human history. Professor Peter Clarke sets out the beliefs of some of these movements and their understanding of the millennium.

Howard Cooper writes as a psychotherapist and a Jew. If the press has taken over from the pulpit, it could be argued that psychotherapy has taken over from the confessional. But Rabbi Cooper believes that the insights of psychotherapy can be of real benefit to religion. As human beings we inevitably project on to God what we most want or most fear. Psychotherapy enables us to take back these projections and recognize them in ourselves. This includes recognizing our capacity for love, goodness, justice, mercy and compassion. A mature religion needs to move beyond projection to a full assumption of human responsibility. So he offers a resounding two cheers and is perhaps even tempted to offer a third.

One of the stereotypes that besets the West, as far as Islam is concerned, is the idea that Muslims have of the State. According to this Muslims do not rest content until every aspect of economic and political life is controlled by Muslims who are guided by Shariah law. Mohammed Abdul Jabbar shows that Muslim thinking on the relationship between religion and society is in fact as varied and as complex as anything in Christianity. In particular there is a profound recognition in many authoritative Islamic sources, that the State is a frail human institution, governed by fallible human beings. It is not legitimate therefore to talk about a divinely approved or regulated State. Together with this there is a recognition of the potential tyranny of all governments, whether Muslim or not and the need for built-in safeguards against this. So whilst he would not want to go all the way with the secular State he is clear that a theocracy, a State that is dominated by those ruling in the name of religion is not something that Islam either wants or could regard as properly Islamic.

Julia Neuberger is unequivocal in her condemnation of the way organized religion, in its Jewish, Christian and Muslim forms, has marginalized women. Religion itself, in its pure form, its aspiration for God and its longing for a universal love, is fundamental to what it is to be a human being. Nothing wrong with that, indeed everything right with it. But religion as we know it has been organized by men, for men, with little account of the dignity and feelings of women. No cheers for that.

Karen Armstrong was once a nun, so she knows what the religious life is like from the inside. Since leaving her convent, however, she has brought a dispassionate eye to the religions of the world. In her essay she is concerned particularly with evil and the threat it poses to all human values and all religious faiths. The religions of the world have devoted too much time and energy on inessentials and too little on solving the multiple problems which beset humanity. Their role, like that of the secularist should be 'to cultivate a sense of life's irreducible mystery, especially as this is revealed to us in other suffering human beings.'

Richard Harries argues that the most important objections today are not philosophical but moral. What religion puts before people too often strikes them as morally crude or insensitive. On the other hand religion, properly understood, has an 'enchantment', that motivates and inspires like nothing else. So secularism, despite its important insights, can only ever bring forth two cheers.

John Mortimer has a rather more sympathetic approach to the values espoused by religion. He much admires many aspects of religious teaching and especially Jesus Christ. Only he is unable to believe in God. So he calls himself a founder member of the Atheists for Christ Society. His two cheers seem to be directed primarily to religion, in the Christian form in which he has received it, even though he himself cannot believe in God.

Our hope is that this book, written from a variety of standpoints, atheist, agnostic and religious and from within religion, from Judaism, Christianity and Islam, will provoke people to be more critical both about the alleged secularism of our times and also of our received religious heritage. We have to make up our own minds. We have no other option. But the contributors to this volume could go beyond this in agreeing that this freedom of choice is not just a necessity but a blessing. And this, I suppose, is why we would all, or nearly all, want to give two cheers for secularism. For the emphasis upon the liberty and profound responsibility of individual choice, is one of the most significant consequences of secularization.

Richard Harries, Bishop of Oxford
Rabbi Sidney Brichto
January 1998

– 1 –
THE RISE OF SECULARIZATION AND THE PERSISTENCE OF RELIGION

Anthony Russell is the author of four books on social change in the countryside and its impact on the rural church. He has been Bishop of Dorchester since 1988. Previously he was Director of the Arthur Rank Centre at the National Agricultural Centre; a member of the Archbishop's Rural Commission and lectured in Sociology at Birmingham and Oxford Universities.

Anthony Russell
Bishop of Dorchester

TWO CHEERS FOR SECULARISM

IN POPULAR USAGE, the word secular, which is often used to describe contemporary society, carries a variety of meanings. For some it is a term of approval indicating that modern society has loosed itself from the thraldom of antiquated and irrational belief; by contrast, for others, it is a shorthand term for all that is perceived to be wrong in modern society: its lack of values and morals, its lack of a sense of community and common purpose. For many, the terms religious and secular are opposed, as if the advance of the latter was responsible for the decline of the former.

The original Latin meaning of the word secular was 'that which belongs to its own time' and it was used to describe the ancient festivals, the hymns and rituals of the Roman world held at long but regular intervals. Later it came to mean 'that which is concerned with the affairs of this world'. Thus, from the twelfth century onwards the term secular is used to describe the parish clergy in distinction to the regular clergy, those who were members of religious orders and lived according to a rule.

Although secularism as a concept has a long history, the term was first used in about 1850 by G.J. Holyoake (who spent six months in prison for public blasphemy before his death in 1906) to denote a system which seeks to interpret and order life on principles taken wholly from the world, without recourse to belief in God and the future life. For Holyoake, it was 'the doctrine that morality should be based on regard to the well-being of mankind in the present life, to the exclusion of all considerations drawn from belief in God or a future state'.[1]

Despite its origins, the term secularization is notoriously difficult to define and it is customarily used to describe a broad process of change in modern society whereby the role and significance of religious thought and practice diminishes both for the individual and for society as a whole. Whilst historians have identified the process of secularization as at work in every age (even in the Old Testament),[2] it is customarily regarded as the product of developments in science and rational thought in the nineteenth century which subsequently became a part of popular culture.

Whilst the notion existed that society was part of a cosmic structure and that its forms and patterns were part of a divine plan, it remained resistant to social enquiry. However, in the mid and late nineteenth century it was demonstrated that society was a human construct and that in many of its aspects religion was a form of social practice. Following Durkheim, it became axiomatic to regard that social practice as having social functions which could be demonstrated.[3]

---

1   Edwards, David, *Religion and Change* (1969) p. 15.
2   Habgood, John, *Church and Nation in a Secular Age* (1983), p. 27. See also Gilbert, A.D, *The Making of Post-Christian Britain* (1980) p. 17 ff.
3   Durkheim, Emile. *The Elementary Forms of the Religious Life* (English tr. 1976).

The comparative study of primitive societies by social anthropologists sought to demonstrate that the functions of religion could be seen in terms of explanation (making sense of the universe); authorisation (the legitimation of leadership roles) and the maintenance of social cohesion (the word religion means to bind in Latin).

At the same time, Herbert Thomas Buckle's *History of Civilisation* (1857), Herbert Spencer's *First Principles* (1862) and W.E.H. Lecky's *History of the Rise and Influence of the Spirit of Rationalism* (1865) all contained the same message: that an advanced society needed to free itself from the dominance of traditional metaphysics and theology which were being swept away as 'dogmatic' and 'unscientific' by the process of civilization. It was argued that if the functions of religion were those of explanation, authorisation and social cohesion, then as other agencies came to fulfil these roles, so religion ceased to be of significance in advanced society. For many students of society, to explain was to explain away; and it was thought that religion would become a social redundancy in advanced society.

The sociologist Ferdinand Tönnies constructed two ideal types of social relationship.[4] The ideal type of the homogeneous, small scale, cohesive kinship group, to which he gave the name *Gemeinschaft*, or community, and which accorded in many of its essential features with the traditional pre-industrial English village. The other ideal type, *Gesellschaft*, or association, is the characteristic form of modern industrial society based on the division of labour and physical and social mobility. In the former, church and community were coterminous and religion, its institutions and its officers, dominated all aspects of civic and personal life. In such a society there was no distinction between a crime and a sin.

Structural differentiation is one of the principal features of a modern society. It is the process by which different aspects of society gain their own autonomy and authority. As a consequence of structural differentiation, religion ceases to be the overarching interpreter and authoriser of all social action but becomes one aspect of an increasingly complex pluralistic society. In such a society religion is seen as an increasingly individual (rather than social) matter and religious practice as a matter of personal choice and preference. From the 1960s, the term secularization was used to describe this process whereby social control, law, medicine, education, and all aspects of commerce and government ceased to be controlled by religious institutions and their officers.[5]

The secularization hypothesis is particularly associated with the 1960s and 1970s and with the name of Dr Bryan Wilson, whose book *Religion in Secular Society* (1966) described secularization as a process which manifests itself in the gradual

---

4   Tönnies, Ferdinand, *Gemeinschaft und Gesellschaft* (1887) (tr. C.P. Loomis Community and Association, 1955).

5   Russell, Anthony, *The Clerical Profession* (1980).

diminution of both the quantity and social significance of religious thinking, practice and institutions in advanced society.[6]

According to Wilson, the decline in church membership and the marginalization of the church as an institution resulted from the effect of changes in thought during the nineteenth century associated with Darwin, Marx and Freud. As a consequence, religion became increasingly implausible to a large section of the population and as they ceased to believe, so they withdrew from membership of the church and the long period of declining church attendance commenced. Owen Chadwick pointed to the difficulties, ambiguities and uncertainties of describing the way in which these changes affected popular thought in the nineteenth century, but he concluded: 'I do not think it is an abuse of such a term to call this radical process, still in part so obscure to the enquirer, and possibly in part undefinable, by the name of secularization ... '.[7] Peter Berger has viewed it in more structural terms as the process whereby religious institutions in an increasingly secular world assume the status of 'deviant, cognitive minorities'. Thus, for all these writers, secularization started as a crisis of religious belief by which, as Berger wrote: 'the plausibility structure of religion was undermined' and became a crisis of religious practice and of religious institutions.[8]

Many nineteenth century social thinkers came to see the Enlightenment as a process which released both individuals and society from the oppressive and all-embracing dominance of religion. The emergence of the State as a secular reality was one of the principal consequences of the Reformation and the religious wars that followed it. Man was portrayed as a radical being able to make appropriate decisions about his and society's future on the basis of empirical facts and his growing knowledge of the workings of the material world.[9] By its nature, Protestantism, with its positive attitude towards the creation of wealth and the development of scientific discovery, represented a significant impetus to a secular reinterpretation of the world and society. In an increasingly advanced society, where scientific (and particularly medical) discoveries made life less unpredictable, where man no longer felt himself to be wholly at the mercy of capricious powers and in need of explanation and reassurance, religion was increasingly portrayed as sustaining unscientific explanations of the physical world or as a supporter of oppressive socio-political systems and means of social control.[10]

---

6 Wilson, B.R., *Religion in Secular Society: a sociological comment* (1966). See also *Contemporary Transformations in Religion* (1976) and *Religion in Sociological Perspective* (1982).

7 Chadwick, Owen, *The Secularisation of the European Mind in the Nineteenth Century* (1975) p. 265.

8 Berger, Peter, *A Rumour of Angels* (1969) p. 47. *See also* Berger, Peter and Luckmann, Thomas, *The Social Construction of Reality* (1966).

9 Gilbert, A.D. ibid., p. i.

10 Davies, Charles, *Religion and the Making of Society* (1994) p. 121 ff.

THE RISE OF SECULARIZATION AND THE PERSISTENCE OF RELIGION

Bryan Wilson, in describing the process of secularization, observed that in modern society people act less in response to religious motivation or direction as they assess the world in empirical and rational terms and base their actions on such assessments. The world has become demystified and desacralized, and people are involved in rational organizations and roles in which, even if they may hold religious views, such views do not provide the basis for judgement or action. Everyday thinking has become instrumental, matter of fact, and life is determined by 'cause and effect' thinking, if only because man knows much more about the workings of the social and physical world. Debates about social questions are dominated not by people representing religious institutions but by people with the appropriate practical knowledge and organizational understandings. Whilst opinions may differ about the nature and function of religious institutions in America, Wilson and others argued that it would be hard to sustain an argument that the development of contemporary American society had been dramatically different from European society on the basis of the fact that there was a much higher level of church attendance in America. He argues that in an advanced society, religious ideas have not so much been replaced by a secular ideology but transformed from within. The churches themselves, particularly in America, he observed, are highly influenced by the secular agenda and operate in a way which is indistinguishable from other voluntary secular organizations. Wilson noted a number of examples where doctrinal stances appear to have been modified or significantly changed in order to prevent religious institutions from losing membership.[11]

The recent history of religious institutions in England (and most European countries) has been significantly different from that of America. Religious institutions, it is argued, have lost membership as their functions have been taken over by other elements of society. As a consequence, religious institutions have become marginal to the mainstream of English society although their long history has served to obscure this fact from many. However, in 1974 the Bishop of Wakefield wrote: 'The time is upon us when a man who involves himself with the Church, who practises his faith in the common ways of life – will do so against the conventions of society'.[12] In England, church leaders have regarded leisure and recreational activities as a direct threat to the church (in a way that is not paralleled in America) and Bishop Randall Davidson devoted part of his charge to the clergy of his diocese of Winchester in 1899 to observing that the bicycle was having a particularly deleterious effect on Sunday church attendance.[13] Sport in particular (which attracts significantly more media coverage than religious institutions though the number of

---

[11] Wilson, B.R. ibid., p. xvi.
[12] Quoted by Gilbert, A.D., ibid., p. xi.
[13] Russell, Anthony, *The Country Parson* (1993) p. 118.

people attending football matches on a Saturday is only a sixth of the number of people attending church services on a Sunday) may be seen in this light as providing some of the traditional functions of integration, cohesion and shared values formerly provided by religious institutions.

The secularization hypothesis suggests that the erosion of the plausibility of religion and the consequent decline in popular religiosity leads inevitably to a decline in the strength of religious institutions and eventually to a religionless society. It is unnecessary to quote the figures which can be found in Robert Currie, Alan Gilbert and Lee Horsley's *Churches and Churchgoers: Patterns of Church Growth in the British Isles since 1700* (1977), which documents in considerable detail the decline in English church attendance.[14] Among other factors, what is of interest is the similarity in the pattern of decline in all denominations, a fact which by itself might support the secularization hypothesis as a master trend in society. Whilst Currie's book is principally concerned with the Free Church and Church of England, the decline has been as significant in the Roman Catholic Church (often thought to be more resistant to secularization). Between 1966 and 1992 there has been a 38% drop in Mass attendance from 2.1 million to 1.3 million. In the Roman Catholic Church in America there were 49,000 seminarians in 1965, in 1992 there were 5,000, in 1960 there were 200,000 nuns and by 1992 this figure had been halved. So significant are social factors in the growth or decline of churches that Currie suggests that these are in every case of greater significance than the internal policies adopted by the churches.

Also, sociologists have observed that one of the effects of the secularization process has been to remove religious institutions and their representatives from the mainstream of national life. The marginalization of the churches is a consequence of structural differentiation in which the public frame of religious symbolism loses its hold and religion becomes almost exclusively a private and personal matter. As in a plural society, where churches have to compete with other leisure organizations for membership, so they experience a process of destructuration as they abandon older forms and procedures in an attempt to maintain membership and are transformed into organizations which are at many points similar to other voluntary associational organizations. Destructuration in the churches may be seen as an attempt to accommodate religious institutions to a pluralistic society in which opinions are framed and transmitted by the media. In such a situation, where religion as such is perceived as losing social significance, religious institutions may reinterpret their role in terms of a wide variety of alternative priorities which typically embrace social work and political activity.

---

14 Currie, Robert, Gilbert, A.D. and Horsley, Lee, *Churches and Churchgoers: Patterns of Church Growth in the British Isles since 1700* (1977).

THE RISE OF SECULARIZATION AND THE PERSISTENCE OF RELIGION

In the late 1960s and early 1970s it was common to portray secularization as a master concept, the workings of which would inevitably sweep away religion or relegate it to the margins of society. However, even then, there were some who were not convinced that secularization was an irreducible process sweeping all religious thinking and practice before it. Possibly the first to signal his disenchantment with the theory of secularization was David Martin who wrote an essay entitled 'Towards the elimination of the concept of secularization', in which he stated: 'I do not regard secularization as involving a more or less unified syndrome of characteristics subject to an irreversible master trend ... the foundations of such master trends are rooted in an ideological view of history.'[15]

The critics of secularization have observed that the process of change from primitive religious societies to modern secular societies appears to assume if not a 'golden age' of religion, then at least a religious baseline from which the process of decline can be measured. Whilst it is possible to observe that religion played a more public and prominent role in a close-knit, isolated, agrarian village culture as opposed to that of a diffuse, anonymous urban society and that secularization is linked to the processes of modernization, nevertheless it would be problematic to support a theory which propounded a straight line progression from a religious traditional society to a secular modern society. The work of recent historical research has made the intensity of the religious condition of the medieval past less easy to believe in and harder to prove. Historians have recently shown that traditional society was more secular and more modern than had been described in the writings such as Huizinga's.[16] Historians such as Macfarlane have described late medieval society as being commercially aggressive, self-confident and expansionist and as a society in which the rights and privileges of individuals, the division of labour and a degree of social mobility were already firmly established.[17] Nor can secularization be seen as an uninterrupted linear process, Adrian Hastings, for instance, describes the eighteenth-century Church of England as being 'profoundly secularized'. He sees English religious history as comprising a series of waves of religious enthusiasm which reached their peaks in the tenth, thirteenth, seventeenth and nineteenth centuries.[18]

Furthermore, the critics of secularization have pointed to a number of other difficulties, not least the fact that the theory appears to draw exclusively on European evidence. The secularization hypothesis is less able to account for the up-

---

15 Martin, David, *The Religious and the Secular* (1969) p. 9 ff. See also *A General Theory of Secularisation* (1978), *The Dilemmas of Contemporary Religion* (1978), *The Breaking of the Image: a Sociology of Christian Theory and Practice* (1980).

16 Huizinga, J., *The Waning of the Middle Ages* (1924) p. 172 ff.

17 Macfarlane, Alan, *The Origins of English Individualism* (1978) p. 168.

18 Hastings, Adrian, *A History of English Christianity 1920–1985* (1986) p. 669 ff.

surge of fundamentalism in the 1980s among Protestant churches in South America. In Brazil there are now more Protestant church attendees than Catholic. The rise of Islamic fundamentalism, the *fatwa* pronounced on Salman Rushdie, the conflagration at Wako in Texas, and the Hebron massacre, together with the role that religion plays in contemporary conflicts in the Middle East, in Northern Ireland and in Bosnia all set question marks against the secularization hypothesis.

At the same time, from an early stage, Martin observed the persistence of irrational and non-scientific views about life.[19] It is hard to regard a society as secular where a breakfast-time television station has a resident astrologer, where horoscopes are printed in many papers. In France, it is reported, that there are 40,000 professional astrologers (more numerous than the clergy) and many business directors employ their services. In Renan's words: 'The gods only go away to make places for other gods'. A part of the paradox of contemporary religion is the way in which educated and intelligent people appear to give credence to a wide range of beliefs that come from astrology, magic, neo-paganism and a whole range of 'new age' beliefs. In the absence of a single public framework of religious belief and symbolism, people turn to the worship of idols, ideologies, principalities and powers which inevitably crowd into the vacuum.

Perhaps the most significant change in contemporary religious life has been the recognition that there are widespread indications that the long years of decline in the mainstream denominations has been arrested. In the Church of England it would seem that the steady decline of the 1960s and 1970s was finally halted in 1987. In 1991 the normal Sunday attendance figure averaged at 1,137,000 or 24 per thousand of the population; a figure which has remained unchanged since 1987. Christmas communicants in 1991 rose by 2% and the total Confirmation figure in 1992 rose by 4% on the previous year. In 1991 a survey of practising Christians by the Independent Television Commission showed that 42% claimed to be Church of England. A survey by Marc Europe in the previous year showed that the baptized membership of the Church of England in the United Kingdom was 26,855,000. Recent debates about the monarchy, the contents of religious education and the appropriate way of celebrating the Normandy landings have made it clear that, for a significant majority, Christianity remains the language of grief and gratitude in society.

Of the many changes to the religious landscape since the 1970s, the two changes that are most difficult to reconcile with the secularization hypothesis are the growth in new religious movements and the rise of fundamentalism. To some commentators, these are seen as a reaction to and a consequence of secularization; to others they are seen as evidence of the persistence of religion, though in a changed and different guise.

---

19 Martin, David, *A Sociology of English Religion* (1967) p. 52 ff.

THE RISE OF SECULARIZATION AND THE PERSISTENCE OF RELIGION

Without doubt, since the 1970s there has been a significant rise in the number of new religious movements and in public interest in the occult, magic and a wide range of beliefs and practices, often referred to as 'new age'. London bookshops now have more books on these subjects than they do on mainstream theology and their influence on popular culture, both at the level of belief, and in the practice of alternative therapies, is widespread. Without doubt, the rise of fundamentalism represents another significant challenge to the secularization hypothesis. Within the last ten years fundamentalist ideas have penetrated and transformed many Muslim countries and a number of world strategists regard fundamentalism as representing the most significant threat to the stability of international order. In Europe it can be noted that many churches have moved away from the more liberal theological positions of the 1970s and 1980s towards more conservative stances influenced by their more fundamentalist (in some churches charismatic) members. This is noticeable in all churches, including the Roman Catholic church where absolutist attitudes to ethical questions, particularly birth control, have been strongly enunciated by Pope John Paul II. On this issue common ground has been established with Muslim fundamentalists at the United Nations Population Conference in Cairo in 1993.

Thus it can be seen that in the face of the persistence, some would argue the recovery, of religion in the 1990s, it is difficult to support the secularization hypothesis as an irreducible process in modern society. It appears that religion is stronger and more persistent, and in England particularly there has been confusion between secularization and deChristianization.[20] Without doubt, the churches have had their position considerably weakened in recent decades both by loss of membership and by the perception that they are marginal to the mainstream concerns of contemporary society. However, the representation of this country as a multi-cultural, multi-faith society has served to accelerate and exaggerate this process, particularly in education, where traditional biblically-based instruction has given way to comparative religion with the implication that religion is a matter only of personal preference and choice. *Social Trends* (24) states that in 1992, out of 58 million people in Great Britain, there were just over half a million Muslims and a quarter of a million Sikhs. There were 140,000 Hindus, 350,000 Jews and 80,000 others. Members of mainstream non-Christian religions represent 1.9% of the total population. By contrast, 46% of the population claim membership of the Church of England (a drop of only 3% since 1970). The Roman Catholic church remained constant at 10%. 65% of the total population of the United Kingdom say that they affirmed a Trinitarian religion.

Contemporary observers of religious practice, particularly parish clergy, have always felt ambivalent about the secularization hypothesis. On the one hand, whilst

---

20 Gilbert, A.D. ibid., p. 102 ff.

it is clear from their own experience that religion has become marginal to the mainstream of social life and action and the clergyman's role is no longer so central to English society, on the other hand, parish clergy are aware of the phenomenon of 'vicarious religion', the mechanism whereby people need others to believe things of which they themselves may not be so certain. There is a widespread recognition that those who attend church are in a sense only the tip of a much larger iceberg and that those who do not attend seem to need to know that the church is there; they need to know that it is available to help them at particular points in the life cycle and to provide a language in which they can interpret the moments of birth and death, of love and the loss of love. Vicarious religion has a long tradition in English history dating back to the masses celebrated by medieval priests on behalf of those who were not present. The outcry which greets expressions of belief by church leaders which are not regarded as orthodox or the possible closure of a church building indicates something of the significance of this phenomenon.

At the same time, parish clergy are aware that those who withdraw from church membership rarely do so because of intellectual doubts; their reasons are more often social. For instance, those who have recently moved from a community in which church-going was a mainstream social activity to an anonymous urban area are less likely to re-establish their contact with the church. It used to be said that Paddington Station was the most religious place in London because it was there that the Welsh, who migrated to the capital, left their religion.

One of the most significant contributions to the secularization debate in recent years is Professor Robin Gill's book *The Myth of the Empty Church* (1993) in which he has demonstrated in considerable detail that decline in churchgoing has many causes, but most of them are social rather than intellectual.[21] He particularly cites the competitive building of churches in the nineteenth century, when, between 1800 and 1850 Welsh non-conformity built a new chapel every eight days.[22] In rural England, church building and renovation reached its peak when the population was already in rapid decline. The declining position of religion in England is a more complex phenomenon than a direct response to the intellectual questions posed by Darwin, Freud and Marx during the nineteenth century. Gill particularly cites the American evidence and suggests that the suburban middle classes in England, which have been most resistant to the impact of secularization, should, according to the proponents of the secularization hypothesis, have shown evidence of decline at an earlier date as one of the earliest areas affected by scientific and rational thought.

It is important to be aware of the danger of '-ism' words in intellectual history; they are a form of shorthand and tend to obscure important distinctions. They are

---

21 Gill, Robin, *The Myth of the Empty Church* (1933). See also *Theology and Social Structure* (1977) and *Beyond Decline: a challenge to the churches* (1988).

22 Thomas, Terence (ed.) *The British: their religious beliefs and practices 1800–1986* (1988) p. 187.

often coined for the purpose of dismissing or ridiculing belief or doctrine worthy of more careful examination. Such words are often loaded with unexamined intellectual content, masquerading as neutral descriptions of an observable and inevitable social process. Without doubt, for some, secularization has been a war-cry of a counter-religious ideology.

There is enough evidence to suggest that the secularization hypothesis may at least be considered as an oversimplification. The view that religion belongs to the past, that modernity is in principle religionless and that modern man must be an atheist is harder to sustain today than it was in the 1960s when the secularization hypothesis was first described. Today, there is a tendency to refer to modern society as being not secularized but religiously pluralistic. The situation of religion in modern society is complex and as yet not wholly satisfactorily described by the sociology of religion. That it has changed, that the secularization hypothesis is an appropriate description of some elements of that change, is clear. However, it would seem that it is not possible to suggest, particularly on the basis of contemporary evidence, that secularization can be regarded as a unilinear master trend, as some of its early proponents suggested, which will lead ultimately to a secular religionless society. The structural forms of religion are adapting and changing to the challenges of a modern pluralistic society and it is these changes that are examined in the subsequent chapters.

– 2 –

JUDAISM IN A SECULAR WORLD

Sidney Brichto is a rabbi, preacher and controversial Jewish thinker. He is Director of the Joseph Levy Foundation and Senior Vice-President of the Union of Liberal and Progressive Synagogues of which he was Director for twenty-five years. He is also a visiting lecturer at the Oxford Centre for Hebrew and Jewish Studies. He is the author of *Funny ... you don't look Jewish - A Guide to Jews and Jewish Life.*

SIDNEY BRICHTO

BEFORE being interviewed for admission to rabbinical college, I sought advice on the sort of questions I might have to face. I was particularly worried they would quiz me about my belief in God; but I was told not to worry because the panel tended to avoid such questions. It appeared that when one rabbinical candidate had been asked whether he believed in God, the Dean of the Hebrew Union College had snorted: 'Now what kind of a question is that?'

Perhaps it was this kind of introduction to the rabbinate which made me more open-minded to the non-believers in our society. My upbringing as a Jew in the United States of America led me to appreciate that there was no conflict between Jewish and secular values. Indeed, the separation of Church and State as enshrined in the American Constitution was to protect the freedom of religion, and not to discourage its hold on the lives of its citizens.

My studies in religion in general and in Judaism in particular have led me to the conclusion that Western secularism is built on the foundations of the Jewish and Christian concepts of God and humanity which had incorporated the genius of Greek and Hellenist thought. As a rabbi, my concern is that while the secular West continues to build on these foundation stones, Western religions seem to be suffering from arrested growth and a loss of the inspiration which first motivated its founders. But I will say more of this later in the essay when I will give illustrations of areas in which secularism has morally transcended religion.

The Bishop of Dorchester, Anthony Russell, has helped by reminding us that it was G.J. Holyoake who first used the term secularism to 'denote a system which seeks to interpret and order life on principles taken wholly from the world, without recourse to belief in God and a future life'. He quotes Holyoake's definition of secularism as 'the doctrine that morality should be based on regard for the well-being of mankind in the present life, to the exclusion of all considerations drawn from belief in God or a future state'. The increasing popularity of this doctrine and its implementation by Western societies has led to an unfortunate combativeness between religion and secularism. The religious often accuse secularists of being godless, and the secularists condemn the religious as prejudiced, totalitarian, and superstitious.

Close scrutiny would show that there is no logical contradiction between secularism as defined by Holyoake and religion. Secular governments will pass legislation without reference to the Bible, but that does not proscribe the possibility that members of their government will not have been influenced by its teaching to come to their decision, or that the whole basis of social welfare, for example, is rooted in previous parliaments which believed that they were heeding the admonitions of God when they instituted laws to look after those who were disadvantaged by reason of circumstances.

Of course, there will be conflict when religions seek to make religious ritual as well as moral law the basis of government. There will also be conflict when good people who are not believers are publicly condemned as sinners, or when humanists seek to remove all vestiges of religious faith from public life. The State of Israel and Arab nations are suffering deep conflicts because their orthodox sections feel that it is their right to impose ancient laws on the community.

Interestingly, while Christianity has maintained that the only way for salvation is through faith in Christ, it was Jesus who first advocated the separation of Church and State, when he said, 'render unto Caesar what is Caesar's and to God what is God's'. But also, in St Paul's mission to the pagan world, he rejected the laws of the Torah, but insisted that believers in Christ must both keep its essential moral laws and the laws of their governments.

But, Judaism too, while demanding obedience to the Torah, through the belief in an oral law given at Sinai, allowed constant reinterpretation to meet the needs of the time, not only as Holyoake would insist, disregarding 'all considerations drawn from belief in God', but even in opposition to God, as the following rabbinic tale indicates:

> The sages had a dispute with Rabbi Eliezer whether a certain oven was susceptible to ritual defilement. On that day, he brought forward every conceivable argument to prove that it was not, but they were not persuaded.
> Finally, he said to them, 'If the Law agrees with me, let this carob tree prove it.' Immediately the tree was flung a hundred cubits away where it took root. They said to him, 'A carob tree proves nothing.' He then said, 'If the Law agrees with me, let this stream prove it.' The stream began to flow backwards. 'A stream proves nothing,' was their response. Then he said, 'If the Law agrees with me, let the walls of the Academy prove it.' The walls of the Academy began to lean over. Rabbi Joshua cried out to them, 'What business is it of yours when the Sages dispute the Law?' Rabbi Eliezer spoke once more, 'if the Law agrees with me, let Heaven prove it.' A divine voice was heard, 'Why do you argue with Rabbi Eliezer when the Law agrees with him in every case.' Rabbi Joshua protested, 'It [the Law] is not in Heaven' (*Deuteronomy*) and we take no notice of divine voices because long ago at Mount Sinai, you wrote in the Torah, One follows the majority.' (*Exodus 23*)
> Rabbi Nathan met the prophet Elijah and asked him, 'What did the Holy One do at that moment?' Elijah answered, 'He laughed joyously and said, "My children have defeated me, my children have defeated me."'
> *The Babylonian Talmud, Tractate Bava Matziah 89*

Furthermore, the Rabbinic Masters affirmed that for Jews living under foreign rule or in the Diaspora, 'The law of the government is the law!'

The nature of Judaism, more so than Christianity, is in sympathy with the secular spirit which is to separate law from religious faith. An oft quoted narrative from the Palestinian Talmud concludes with God saying about his sinning children: 'Would that they had forsaken me but kept my Torah.' The Torah which God gave His people in order for them to teach mankind, was designed to establish the same order on earth as He had in the heavens. The concluding sentence of the Kaddish, one of Judaism's central prayers, reads: 'He who makes peace in his heavens, let Him make peace for us and for all Israel.' Jesus expressed a similar sentiment when he advised to his disciples how to pray: 'Our Father which art in heaven, hallowed be thy name. Thy Kingdom come, thy will be done, on earth as it is in heaven.' The Torah is about establishing the law of God on earth.

Since the Torah was designed for this world rather than for the heavens, it is essentially 'secular', in its original sense of 'associated with this age' rather than with eternity. To this extent, the goal of enlightened secularists is no different from that of Jews, or adherents of any religion whose priorities lie in the promotion of general happiness for all members of the human race. Because this is so, I have always felt that I am a 'secularist' and that Judaism is a 'secular' religion.

The secular nature of Judaism confuses anyone – Jew as well as non-Jew – who believes that religions must be spiritual by nature. For this reason they are more comfortable with the picture of those Jews who still dress in the garb of the 17th-century Polish aristocracy – the Hasidim with their beards and earlocks – because they appear as other-worldly, which is the image people identify with religious faith. But most Jews are not like them, and most Jews, including the modern orthodox, consider themselves as part of the secular world. But they also identify religion with belief in salvation and a hereafter, they too are confused about the philosophy of Judaism. At a dinner party recently I heard a Jewish businessman complaining that while almost any Catholic, Protestant or Muslim could explain his or her beliefs, most Jews could not, and he argued that it was because they had none! I suggested to him that his non-spiritual Jewish identity was not unusual, but the norm. I took the opportunity to explain the basis of Judaism. The ten principles of Judaism which I have enlarged for the purpose of this essay indicate the secular nature of the Jewish faith. Judaism believes:

1 The life we live now is all that really counts. No after-life can be an excuse for not making the most of this life, no after-life can compensate for suffering in this life.

2 Life is good with an obligation to enjoy it, but not at the expense of someone else's enjoyment. Moses said to the people of Israel in the name of God: 'I have put before you life and death, choose life and live'.

3 The purpose of the Torah, the Divine Teaching, is to create rules to prevent individuals from hurting each other. 'Do not do unto others what is hateful to you', is what Hillel said to the would-be convert: 'This is the whole Torah – the rest is commentary – now go and study!'

4 The individuals' happiness is dependent on the health of their society. Individuals have a responsibility to their community because their own security is dependent upon it. Hurting the community is hurting oneself; helping it is

helping oneself. There can be no personal salvation without collective salvation. Jews on the holiest day of the year, Yom Kippur, repent collectively: 'We are all sinners; we have all behaved dishonestly ... '

5   Humans are social animals – they need to relate to each other to achieve completeness and happiness. Hillel said: 'If I am not for myself, who will be, but if I am only for myself, what am I?'

6   We keep laws so long as we know that they are in our own interest. By breaking them we achieve short-term pleasures but lose long-term happiness. Good people achieve contentment. Bad people enjoy thrills, but lose out on the joy of lasting and fulfilling relationships.

7   Repentance and forgiveness are possible when a person alters his or her behaviour. God does not want the death of the sinner, but a return to Him and life.

8   The human spirit is immortal. To reinforce the value of each individual the Rabbinic Masters decided that the individual spirit returns to God after death, that the good person lives in the light of the divine presence forever, and that the bad person is deprived of that light and lives in eternal isolation.

9   God is involved in the future of humanity; He is the guarantor of the value of each human life. 'In the image of God created He Man, male and female He created them'. Each person is an end in itself and should not be used as an object or a means for social experimentation.

10 The ultimate human objective is a world in which God's presence is felt in the harmonious relationships between all humans, as it is already felt in the glory of the beauty and majesty of the natural world.

Because Judaism is of and for this world it is 'secular'; but God is the foundation stone on which morality has developed and in the Jewish view still depends. Sadly, I recognize that the advances in civilization over the last 500 years have been in spite of religious belief and not because of it. Buttressed by concepts of authority, obedience and divine providence, religious institutions made a pact with the governing powers to thwart any change in the status quo which might damage their own position. The freedom of scientific enquiry, the development of Utopian social philosophies, the democratization of human institutions and the freedom of the individual were increased, if at all, by the heretics who challenged those religious dogmas which offered a kingdom in heaven for suffering humanity and neglected to strive towards fulfilling ancient prophetic promises of a kingdom of heaven on earth.

We need only look at contemporary events to see how religions, and I would include Judaism in this, lag behind some of the initiatives taken by enlightened governments. Was it Judaism, Christianity, Islam or for that matter the religions of the East which demanded rights for workers, equality for women, and an end to the persecution of homosexuals, or was it democratic parliaments? Was the Welfare State promoted by religious or secular institutions? Whereas most professions have been open to both sexes for decades, orthodox Judaism, the Catholic Church and Islam will not countenance women priests or religious leaders. Other religious authorities are deeply divided on the issue – some realizing how out-of-date they have become but others still interpreting any change as a diminution of spiritual truth and a threat to their integrity as representatives of God on earth. Also, in an overpopulated world, Western and Eastern governments have legislated on the right to control birth, in the face of opposition from most religions.

Democratic secularism has also released individuals from the heavy hand of authoritarianism and of social restrictions based on class and rank while revealed religion, founded on authority and consensus, has historically considered individuality, like freedom of choice, to be a danger. But religion has had to adapt to the popularity of these secular concepts, and religious leaders now often extol the freedom of individuals to choose their own destiny. Nevertheless, the religious fear of this assertion is also apparent, as clergymen, led in Britain by the former and present Orthodox Chief Rabbis, criticize modern society for its emphasis on individual rights rather than on social duties. They are right to warn us against libertarian individualism but these attacks should not be used to justify the power of the community to repress individual freedom. Indeed, few social issues have been the concern of organized religion. Most sensitive people have had to find their opportunities for defending social causes in voluntary organizations rather than through synagogues or churches. The few clergymen who have taken the lead in these activities are notable because they have been the exceptions.

The reason I am prepared to give two but not three cheers for secularism is because the transcendental power called God is, I believe, a requirement in the quest for human redemption. Secularism without a concept of a divine creator generally loses its way, and often causes havoc and destruction. A particularly glaring example is the Nazi movement, whose leaders and ideologies sought to return the world to what they saw as pagan days, when power was its own justification. The Jewish-Christian God was viewed as an evil belief imposed on the strong by the weak in their attempt to inherit the earth by robbing it from men stronger than themselves. Hitler attempted to make power the sole criterion of human behaviour. He enlisted a whole nation in the crusade to kill God and human civilization.

German National Socialism was an extreme aberration of secularism, but was far from unique, as can be seen from the rise and fall of communism in the former Soviet Union and Eastern Europe. On the one hand, Karl Marx was a prophet of universalism, of a classless society and of an end to individual alienation from the environment; on the other hand, the absence of a transcendent principle in *Das Kapital,* the communist Bible, enabled tyrants to achieve and maintain power while experimenting with human beings as though they were armies of ants. They justified the most ruthless policies on the basis that the ends justified the means. Stalin sacrificed twenty million Kulaks for the collectivization of the peasantry, while Mao Tse-Tung destroyed thirty million Chinese in his 'Great Leap Forward'.

If one believes that God created men and women in His own image, then every life is equally precious. As the Rabbinic Masters put it, 'He who saves a life saves a world, and he who destroys a life destroys a world'. Of course, believing in a compassionate God did not dissuade crusaders from killing Jews and Muslims, or the Inquisition from torturing hundreds, if not thousands of 'heretics' to death. Religious institutions, like every other political body, will be subject to corruption; but a capacity for evil in the 'name of God' should not prevent us from acknowledging the dangers of acting as though there is no God. When humanity regards itself as the measure of all things, it loses those standards which affirm the value of every human life.

One must be concerned when democratic secularism begins to lose its moral direction, which seems to be happening. Nationalism grew hand in hand with democratic government. While these national democratic states are sensitive and responsive to the needs of all their citizens, rich or poor, they do not sufficiently extend this altruism beyond their borders. Foreign diplomacy is based on national interest and not on the concept of transnational morality. International laws are accepted only when nations believe it is in their interest to do so.

Governments and institutions in the West have not yet adjusted to advances in computer or communication technology. The world is shrinking and the powers of productivity are greater with a much smaller work force. The need for each nation to keep the competitive edge on its neighbours by producing and selling more has not resolved the problems of unemployment, but has endangered the planet by exhausting its natural resources and polluting its environment. All this is happening against a backdrop of starvation in some parts of the world and a disgracefully minimal standard of living in other parts. Relationships are forged between democratic countries and barbarous dictatorships purely for the economic benefit of the few. This is sowing seeds of discontent among more and more individuals who now have more reason to be anxious for their future happiness than they had fifty years ago.

Admittedly, secularism is 'of this world'. We applaud its success in providing material security to the mass of men and women, in our culture at least, and for the way it has given them freedom and leisure to study, to pursue the arts, to visit foreign places, and to do whatever gives them pleasure. When, however, material wealth becomes an end in itself, and is employed without concern for the sacrifices necessary to achieve it, it takes the place of God and we enter the realm of idolatry. The sense of purposelessness, the indignity caused by the unemployment of people who have been trained to believe that paid work is the greatest good, leads to hopelessness, and this in turn to crime, violence and to family and social breakdown.

The increasing dysfunction of our society can be detected in the 'Back to Basics' call, in the increasingly deep dissatisfaction with our educational system, in the tendency for the government to blame the Churches for the lack of moral leadership, and for the Churches to blame the government for the lack of concern about the most vulnerable people in society. Parents, who have ceased to make the home a moral centre for their children, blame everyone but themselves.

The moral challenges to government and to religious and educational institutions are enormous. For people who believe as I do, the belief in God could play a role in developing positive human relationships based on shared values rather than pleasures that alienate us from our environment and society. But is there an image of God capable of inspiring belief in a secular society? The image of God has been so badly tarnished that among those who have disowned the traditional concept of the Jewish-Christian God are Jewish and Christian ministers. The Jewish Humanist Society in the United States is led by ordained rabbis. The Sea of Faith movement led by Don Cupitt is made up of Christian clergy who cannot square the wickedness of humanity and the suffering in the world with our omnipotent interventionist God. The murder of millions for no other reason than being born as descendants of Jews must have shaken God's heavenly throne. 'Where was God?' Elie Wiesel asked, and the answer still needs to be found if faith in Him is to be rekindled. Nor can non-believers cope with the millions who have been murdered and continue to be slaughtered in the name of God. The fact that most present wars and conflicts are based on religious differences is inescapable and makes the answer to the question of 'What is God?' so necessary.

In responding to this question, I can only speak from my personal interpretation of the Jewish tradition. And I must begin by denying the image of the Jewish God as promoted by some Christians and as accepted by many secularists, even ignorant Jews. The God of the Hebrew Bible has been maligned as one of vengeance, a God who mercilessly punishes those who oppose Him and disobey His laws. But this is a gross travesty of the truth, put about largely by some Christians attempting to prove the superiority of the New Testament over what within Christianity is regarded as the 'Old' Testament.

Contrast this popular view of the 'Old' Testament God with these prophetic verses:

> What are your endless sacrifices to me?
> says Yahweh.
> I am sick of holocausts of rams

and the fat of calves.
The blood of bulls and of goats revolts me.

When you stretch out your hands
I turn my eyes away.
You may multiply your prayers,
I shall not listen.
Your hands are covered with blood,
wash, make yourselves clean.

Take your wrong-doing out of my sight.
Cease to do evil.
Learn to do good,
search for justice,
help the oppressed,
be just to the orphan,
plead for the widow.

Isaiah 1: 11, 15-17

The God whose major concern is social justice is not confined to the latter prophets, but appears in Deuteronomy, the fifth book of Moses: 'He who sees justice done for the orphan and the widow, who loves the stranger and gives him food and clothing'. (*Deuteronomy* 10: 18)

The paradox for believers and non-believers alike is that God's reputation for omnipotence contradicts His perfect goodness. The response that there is no contradiction because humanity has free will is a feeble one because the essence of revealed religion is God's intervention in human affairs, e.g. redeeming the Israelites from Egyptian bondage or, according to Christianity, sending His Son to redeem the world. And if God chose to suspend His law of non-interference on these occasions, why did He not save Jews from Auschwitz or early Christians from martyrdom in Rome? In addition, what of the natural disasters which swallow up the innocent as well as the wicked for which men and women bear no responsibility? If free will is a justification for human evil, how can religious people assert that God guarantees the ultimate victory of the good when it is not up to Him?

A Jewish prayer which is recited three times a day lauds God as, 'He who supports the fallen, heals the sick and frees the captive.' Henry Slonimsky, my own mentor at rabbinical college, used to quote this passage to rabbinical students, and ask, 'Boys, when did He ever *do* it?' By the way, he was the Dean who objected to questions about God being asked of candidates for the rabbinical college. One associate of mine who regularly takes his children to synagogue asked me recently how anyone could believe in a God who actually does 'F... all?' This is not a new question, for when the Romans asked some of the ancient rabbis what the Jewish God did – since He certainly did not bring them victory over their enemies – they replied: 'He arranges marriages'.

The Israelite prophets themselves voiced populist doubts about the 'goodness' of a God who seemed to favour the wicked over the innocent. Malachi tells the people of Israel:

> You have wearied Yahweh with your talk. You ask, 'How have we wearied him?' When you say, 'Any evil-doer is good as far as Yahweh is concerned, indeed he is delighted with them'; or when you say, 'Where is God of fair judgement now?
>
> You have said harsh things about me, says Yahweh. And yet you say, 'What have we said against you?' You have said, 'It is useless to serve God; what is the good of keeping his commands or of walking mournfully before Yahweh Sabaoth? In fact, we now call the arrogant the happy ones; the evil-doers are the ones who prosper; they put God to the test, yet come to no harm!'
>
> Malachi 2: 17; 3: 13–15

In an age when a range of gods were associated with different aspects of nature, it was easy to forsake a God who did not answer one's prayers and to turn to another who had more power or was more favourably disposed to use it on the petitioner's behalf. In our scientific age, it is more usual to negate God as an untenable proposition. But even men and women of deep faith feel the need to cry out against a God who is unable or unwilling to thwart wickedness:

> How long, Yahweh, am I to cry for help
> while you will not listen;
> to cry, 'Violence!' in your ear
> while you will not save?
>
> Why do you make me see wrong-doing,
> why do you countenance oppression?
>
> Plundering and violence confront me,
> contention and discord flourish.
>
> And so the law loses its grip
> and justice never emerges,
> since the wicked outwits the upright
> and so justice comes out perverted.
>
> Habakkuk 1: 1–4

The prophet goes on to question how God can tolerate such evil:

> Your eyes are too pure to rest on evil,
> you cannot look on at oppression.
> Why do you look on at those who play the traitor,
> why say nothing while the wicked swallows someone
> more upright than himself?
>
> Habakkuk 1: 13

The prophets kept faith in God because they saw no other way of injecting meaning into their lives. Bach and Mozart composed sublime music, Shakespeare encompassed human life in words. The genius of prophets such as Amos, Isaiah, Hosea and Jeremiah was to declare the word of God which was within them, a calling they could not resist. He was a fire burning in their hearts.

> You have seduced me, Yahweh, and I have let myself be seduced;
> you have overpowered me: you were the stronger.
> I am a daily laughing-stock,
> everybody's butt.
> Each time I speak the word, I have to howl
> and proclaim: 'Violence and ruin!'
> The word of Yahweh has meant for me
> insult, derision, all day long.
> I used to say, 'I will not think about him,
> I will not speak his name anymore'.
> Then there seemed to be a fire burning in my heart,
> imprisoned in my bones.
> The effort to restrain it wearied me,
> I could not bear it.
>
> *Jeremiah* 20: 7–9

The American philosopher and psychologist, William James, wrote an essay at the turn of the century entitled 'The Will to Believe'. In it he argued that a person who has the firm belief that he can jump over an abyss to save his life is far more likely to succeed than the one who does not. Anyone who believes in a power for goodness, love, hope and charity will be more motivated, and therefore more likely to find the soil in which to plant the seeds of virtue.

However true this may be, it is still quite far from a rational argument for the existence of God. If human need is to be the basis for faith, I prefer the reason given to me by a friend who is a survivor of the Holocaust. He said, 'There has to be a God. With whom else could I be angry?' But if an omnipotent God who is also good has become untenable, it does not rule out the existence of the God who stirred our biblical ancestors and those who followed them. All we need to do is reject the concept of omnipotence. For Henry Slonimsky did not leave his rhetorical question unanswered. When we agreed that God indeed does *not* support the fallen, he retorted: 'Boys, when we do it, He does it'. According to such a view, we are God's partners in creating a better world. Good and courageous people enthrone God; and his kingdom on earth is a vision which only the good and the noble can realize. This partnership between mankind and God was acknowledged by the Rabbinic Masters and nowhere more boldly than in the Midrash in their comments on biblical verses from Isaiah and Psalms.

> 'Ye are my Witnesses saith the Lord, and I am God' (*Isaiah* 43: 12). That is, when ye are my witnesses I am God, and when ye are not my witnesses I am as it were not God.

> 'Unto thee I lift up mine eyes O thou that sittest in the heavens,' says the Psalmist (Psalm 123: 1). 'If it were not for me, i.e., if I did not lift up my eyes, thou O God wouldst not be sitting in the heavens'.
>
> <div align="right">(<i>Sifre Deut</i> § 346)</div>

God can, therefore, be viewed as the creative power for goodness in the world. The goal for God's witnesses is the time when peace and harmony between individuals of all races and peoples are as natural to our world as is the splendour of the stars in their heavenly courses.

> Then the Lord will become King of the whole world. When that Day comes, the Lord will be the One and Only, and His name one name.
>
> <div align="right">(<i>Zechariah</i> 14: 9)</div>

With the belief in a God who redeems spiritually and materially in this world, prayer becomes more than an automatic and formal exercise. God will not be expected to spare one child from leukaemia, while allowing other children to die from the disease. Our prayers will be for the strength to do His work, to generate the resources – human and material – to prevent suffering through research and medical skills, rather than squandering these resources on war and on developing ever more destructive armaments. Without discounting the contribution of Christianity in the quest for a moral world, we should appreciate that the fundamental concept of Judaism is a God who is the source of law and social justice.

Unlike St Paul, Judaism has never despaired of the power of law to transform humans into images of God. For Paul the transformation of the human spirit through faith in the Son of God was the only way towards redemption. But Jews held fast to the belief that human legislation based on the understanding of what God requires of us is more pragmatic. A further consequence of this principle is that Jewish spirituality should be sought less in the lives and writings of Jewish mystics, whose spirituality will be similar to that of mystics of other faiths – but in the absorption of its teachers and students in the study of Torah. The purpose of study is to learn God's will even though we cannot comprehend the nature of his being: 'What does the Lord ask of you? Act justly, love kindness and walk humbly with God.' (*Micah* 6:8)

Atheists and agnostics will protest that I am calling for faith in a God who may not exist, merely because it would help humanity to progress morally, and that what I am suggesting is a form of Pascal's wager. He argued that if you do not believe in God and He exists, you would be the loser. If you believe in him, and he does not exist, you have lost nothing, but if He does exist, you are in a fortunate situation. In a sense, that is true, for if enough humans wanted there to be a God whose divinity became part of them and of their relationships, this God would happen. But, if you feel that this is a disingenuous approach, I would ask, 'Why should not men and women continue to warm their hands at the fires of faith lit by the prophets and saints of all religions who felt inspired by a power outside themselves?' There is great power in art though most cannot paint or compose or even play a musical instrument. Why should people not hear the voice of God in the sacred literature of their ancestors even if they did not hear it themselves? Those who subscribe to no religion need not close their hearts and souls to religious genius simply because it is not their tradition, any more than they should close their minds to Shakespeare because they are not English.

The challenge is to hear the language of spirituality. Were those who cherish the benefits of secularism able to understand what the great religious minds have to offer, we might be offering secularists and their works more than two cheers. Of course, were religious people also to understand and practise their teachings rather than be lost in the morass of rituals and theology, they would draw closer to God those who for moral reasons have decided to keep their distance.

Quotations from the Scriptures come from *The Jerusalem Bible*, Darton, Longman & Todd, London 1968.

– 3 –

WHY AND WHY NOT

Frederic Raphael is the author of twenty novels, four volumes of short stories and two biographies. He has written a number of films and television plays. He is also a regular contributor to *The Sunday Times, Prospect, The New Statesman* and other publications. He was born in Chicago, but has lived most of his life in Europe. He was a Major Scholar in Classics at St John's College, Cambridge, and is a Fellow of the Royal Society of Literature. He is married and has three children.

FREDERIC RAPHAEL

Suppose I say that the body will rot, and another says, 'No. Particles will rejoin in a thousand years, and there will be a Resurrection of you.'
If someone said, 'Wittgenstein, do you believe in this?' I'd say, 'No.' 'Do you contradict this man?' I'd say, 'No.'
If you say this, the contradiction already lies in this.
Would you say: 'I believe the opposite', or 'There's no reason to suppose such a thing'? I'd say neither.

Ludwig Wittgenstein,
Lectures on Religious Belief

TAUTOLOGIES HAVE no appetite; they are satisfied by themselves: the Jewish God is said to have announced himself, on at least one occasion, as 'I am That I am,' a statement which, in English at least, makes Him hard to distinguish, logically, from the Aristotelian deity whose only worthy object of contemplation is himself. In much the same way, the Christian version of the unmoved mover has, in view of his ubiquity, nowhere he could conceivably go. Thales' remark, 'The world is full of Gods' has a monotheistic corollary which is best, if uncomfortably, declared in Spinoza's economic idea of the equivalence of God and Nature: on this reading, God is full of the world, in the sense of Creation, and the Creation *is* God (an argument which sanctifies ecology).

However, Thales' declaration was a prelude not to the kind of superstition still current when Theophrastus satirized it two or three centuries later, but rather to a 'rational' discounting of theological explanations of natural phenomena: since there were gods everywhere, nothing specific could be attributed to their presence. If 'a god is in (or behind) it' was true of everything, it was also irrelevant; all systems which explain everything also explain nothing: 'God's mercy', like 'Allah's will', covers both life and death, but insures neither. Thales' assertion of a multiplicity of gods was at once a preambulatory acknowledgement of divinities' existence and a pious disinclination to include them in practical considerations. (The word 'consideration' has, at its root, the idea of star-gazing, of evaluating heavenly prospects, which illustrates quite prettily how hard, if not impossible, it is to find forms of language untainted by implications which subvert the supposed clarity of their expression.)

When Einstein said that God does not play dice with His creation, he did not assert the futility of science, but its God-backed dependability. The pious may take what comfort they choose from this. However, the amusing solemnity of Einstein's remark hardly endorses any known creed: God here might as well be another name for the governing principle of the universe as for a loving Father. Einstein's evident purpose was to fortify human reliance on intelligence, not to underwrite credulity in, for example, omens, miracles or divine intervention. It was precisely Creation's lack of capricious frivolity on which Einstein was insisting.

In this he had much in common with René Descartes' rather desperate attempt to find a way back from the extreme scepticism into which reason had led him by maintaining that God would not allow man to be systematically misled and that therefore the material world did indeed exist, even though there was no proof that it did. Descartes retrieved the world's reality more or less as Berkeleians did when they made God the eternal observer who, by unsleeping vigilance, made sure that the tree in the quad did not disappear when no mortal was looking at it. All dogmatic dismissals of God have a way of preparing His return; it is for this reason that Wittgenstein's remarks, cited above, have a steady place in the logic of what might be called God-talk.

At the simplest level, it is a notorious truth that the non-existence of God can no more be proved than can His existence. Nor, of course, can the non-existence of the Devil or of the vocal but invisible Virgil to whose views, at critical moments, the classical scholar Jackson Knight had the privilege of listening, thus gaining incontrovertible evidence of what the *Aeneid* was meant to mean.

As E.R. Dodds pointed out, in *The Greeks and the Irrational*, the Greek 'invention' of reason did not mean that they no longer 'believed in' a supernatural dimension to their world, still less that, at the culmination of their civilization, they became the apostles of Reason. The cult of rationality has its nervous appeal only in the light of a consciousness of the danger, and charm, of the irrational. We are reasonable, if we are, *as if we were*; it is both the strength and the hypocrisy of logic and of constitutions, of justice and of compromise, that we *take them to be* valid.

Dodds' crucial example of the stand-off between civility and savagery, between the uses of reason and the seduction of what lay outside it, was Euripides' *Bacchae*, that terrifyingly sane dramatization of supernaturally inspired, frighteningly uncivil madness. It is part of the comedy of scholarship that Euripides' modern fame began with his reputation as a 'rationalist'. He might better be called an ironist. What is most truly modern about him is his (perhaps appalled) recognition of the intimidating force of powers which merely reasonable men cannot accommodate in any practical scheme of political control.

The ultimate 'reasonable' vestige of this kind of uncontrollable force is 'the market', to which Thatcherites wished us to bow in pious impotence. One cannot easily attribute virtue to the market, but its acolytes urge us to yield to its wisdom; it knows best when prices should rise or fall and those who seek to oppose its course, up or down, pay for their impiety with ruin. It is a small step, as totalitarian schemes have proved, from a belief in inevitabilities (which are, at their 'truest', another species of tautology) to a callous determination to be on their side: social Darwinism and Marxism seek to curry favour with the Future by being its deputies. We thus arrive at a paradox: it may be true that nothing can stop what cannot be stopped, if only because it cannot be false, but it does not follow that man has a *moral* obligation to be its partisan. On the contrary, if man's morality is anything of value, it involves the *construction* of generosities which are not necessarily to be found in God or nature (the myth of Prometheus, as Shelley perceived, is an argument on precisely this topic).

If man were *only* one more inhabitant of the earth, like the fox, he would have (and could have) no *conceivable* duty to preserve it. Thus if Nature is synonymous with God, man is the only unnatural – if far from exemplary – mundane being. One way or another, we are on our own. Does this imply that selfishness is more 'natural' (oh that adjective!) than the altruism on which 'community' religions tend to insist? In the Authorised Version, Jesus himself asked only that we love our neighbours *as ourselves.* There was perhaps a measure of self-regard even in him: 'Suffer the little children to come unto *me*' is hardly the remark of a man with markedly low self-esteem.

Those who make programmatic demands for 'more religion' – they range from philosophers such as Iris Murdoch to Christians such as, oh, Pat Buchanan – seem always to imagine, with more or less intelligence or honesty, that children, in particular, can receive injections of religion, in safe doses, as a result of which they will be vaccinated against wickedness without becoming unduly virtuous. The aversion to 'extremism' (especially Muslim) on the part of those who favour the inculcation of 'religious knowledge' is as comic – in its presumption that the love of God can be administered in controlled quantities – as was Pentheus' repudiation of Dionysos. It is possible both to sympathize with those who lament the lost good effects of religion, without being prepared to endorse wholehearted allegiance to it, and to find them laughably ignorant of what immoderate devotion gods regularly demand from their adherents. To give children a little bit of religion is not unlike making a woman a little bit pregnant. But to give them none, what is that?

Bacchae is a cool account of the dangers of repression. The young King Pentheus of Thebes ridicules the pretensions of the 'hippy' vagabond, of ambiguous sexuality, who announces himself to be the god Dionysos. Just as Stalin discounted the influence of the Pope, by asking how many divisions he had, so Pentheus mocks the effete youth who is foolish enough to threaten him. After a period of dangerous patience, the god responds by releasing forces which not only rock the seven-gated city's foundations but later delude King Pentheus himself into putting on drag in order to spy on the orgiastic rituals to which the fugitive women of Thebes have been so excitedly seduced. Finally, Pentheus becomes their prey; mistaken for a wild beast, he is torn to pieces by a female hunting party led by his own mother, after which 'sanity' returns to the city and Dionysos goes calmly, unremorsefully, on his way.

It is part of Euripides' perceptive wit that he makes Tiresias – T.S. Eliot's 'old man with wrinkled dugs', the prophet who has had sexual experience as both a man and as a woman – and Kadmus (the superannuated grandfather of the reigning prince) the advocates of caution, tolerance and, so to speak, elasticity: they advise Pentheus against a violent response to Dionysos' demands that his cult be honoured in the city where his mother, Semele, was born. Pentheus dismisses their prudence and, like any young fogey, announces himself the vessel of an incautious conservatism, contemptuous of the new. Refusal to believe that there can be anything which is not subject to his arbitrary rule brings disaster on the king and on his city. To insist on the *status quo*, we infer, is always a form of tyranny; the exclusion of the Other, of which Dionysos was the apotheosis, leads to the collapse of the Self. Unable to see the divinity of the androgynous hippy who is front of him, Pentheus destroys both himself and his kingdom.

It would be imprudent to draw precise moral or theological conclusions from a play whose 'argument' contains so much irony and is itself a blend of the hot and the cold. As every schoolboy used to know, Euripides wrote *Bacchae*, usually said to be his last play, in Thrace (where Dionysos was particularly venerated), after he, like Anaxagoras, had been exiled from Athens for flagrant heterodoxy. *Bacchae* may ridicule the vanities of a young king, but it is certainly not an unalloyed advertisement for Dionysos, still less an assertion of the 'truth' of the Olympic religion. (The Greeks had no more notion of a formal theology than the Jews.)

If Euripides cannot be shown to have written *Bacchae* with any purpose but to enjoy himself, or perhaps to flaunt his now unbridled genius to the Athenians who expelled him, it is not foolish to contrast his play with Plato's *Republic*, on which, inadvertently or not, it offers sarcastic comment. In *his* masterpiece, Plato implicitly criticized the Olympic gods – even those of unquestionable title in the Greek pantheon – for their immorality, although he was slyly tactful enough to attack Homer and Aeschylus for their irresponsible portraits of the Olympians rather than directly to reproach the gods themselves.

In his denunciation of irresponsible art, Plato maintained that the ideal polity could not allow the gods to be portrayed as lecherous or drunk or dishonest; a revised version of their personal histories would have to be promulgated. (Christians are sometimes embarrassed by the story that Jesus blasted a fig tree, in what seems like a fit of petulance; it is easier to declare the story apocryphal than to admit that Jesus lost control of himself.) The Platonic demand that the gods behave themselves perfectly was expressed in a refusal to allow that they could do anything else; since logically they could not misbehave, they must have been misreported by the poets whose presence in the polity was as undesirable to the philosopher as Dionysos' was to Pentheus or that of 'free-thinking Jews' was to Mr Eliot, when he considered the form which his ideal Christian state should take.

What distinguished the Greek writers of the 5th and 4th centuries was the development of a language – evolving from that of myth – sufficiently commodious both to respect and to question the heroes and gods who supplied the essential furniture of the Greek imagination. If this observation is something of a commonplace, it is less common to point out with what more or less assertive tact Euripides and his contemporaries, including Plato, incorporated what more artless writers might simply have junked. As Wittgenstein recommended, in another context, they 'said the new thing in the old language'; in this way, they sustained the complex continuities of their culture. They rationalized and humanized, what Seferis, more than twenty centuries later, recognized as 'the Greek style' without jettisoning its ballast of unreason and even of savagery. The Jews, in a not wholly different way, preserved the strands of community, even after the catastrophe of Trajan, by distinguishing the specificity of quotidian law from the apocalyptic tradition of the prophets: reason and the irrational are married by their divorce. Defeated Athens and desecrated Jerusalem thus remained, and remain, the poles of European thought, for and against God or gods.

To humanize is not, perhaps unfortunately, to disarm; quite the contrary. The late Gillian Rose's retrieval of violence *within* ethics, within 'polite' (urban) morality, was an attempt to restore the dangerous complexity which 'modernism' disparaged; her awkward, knotty language was the linguistic correlative of the violence which, like Dionysos, had to be admitted into the human audit if it was to render a full inventory of our prospects. The New Testament parable of the Seven Devils warns of the futility of supposing that we can eliminate the diabolical element from human life. Jung maintained that the great mistake of Christian theology was the eviction of the Devil from the Trinity. Those who suppose that they have purged their society of 'the one thing' which threatens its tranquillity procure the circumstances for even greater horrors.

It is difficult to imagine that Mr Eliot understood the relevance of this warning to his plans for a Christian society. As Freud also implies, the unfathomable, the scandalous, is part of what we are; the inadmissible will always find a way in. The notion of a homogeneous and virtuous society sponsors the seven devils – of cruelty, superstition, ignorance, vanity, immobilism, exclusivity, and self-righteousness – which come to replace the domestic devil of, let us say, *dirt*. The 'Victorian' eviction of dirt, in the sexual sense, has given the notion of 'expressing one's sexuality' the commanding significance which, in our time, has sanctioned it to become a, if not *the*, form of salvation. As any ironist might have guessed, the triumph of the pleasure principle leaves people wondering why they cannot be happier still.

So what is all this about? It amounts, I suppose, to a sort of declarative evasion on my part. I have tried, in the form of a discursive intellectual parable, to show how difficult it is for man – let alone *this* man – to find a reasonable language in which to consider (aha!) what God means, or should mean to him. The naive atheist, who sees no reason to believe in a Being who never manifests those qualities of goodness or love which are so regularly attributed to it, can always have scathing fun with the credulities of the faithful, but he is powerless to ignore what he is pleased to disparage. He is not refuted by those who remind him that the battlefield restores many men to piety, any more than he can embarrass the pious by reference to God's callousness when it comes to Auschwitz or to the suffering child. The agnostic is not impressed by the argument *e consensu gentium*, which invites him, democratically, to pious conformity in view of the general human belief in a Supreme Being; nor is the specifically religious man dismayed by the anthropologist's parade of the often congruent varieties of human credulity. Sir James Frazer was one of the first to point out how close were the ideas of savages and of civilized persons; but if he was aware of the Christ-like aspects of Dionysos, he himself remained a complacent Anglican.

The rationalist would like to believe in a relatively simple creation, in which man has no right to arrogate to himself privileges – such as the possession of an immortal soul – which are denied to his dog. It would, in some ways, indeed be nice if everyone were modest enough to accept that he or she is a more or less ephemeral creature, graced with a lease of years by Nature and faced, alas or hurrah, with painless extinction in due course. It would be no less nice if such a doctrine, entirely congruent – it can be argued – with what we actually know, led to a generous, Epicurean, universally amiable world. The problem, as Gillian Rose insisted, is that we cannot be exclusively nice, or reasonable; however sublime our use of it, violence is part of our nature. Its exclusion procures its return. And – as René Girard has argued – from violence, consistent with, and inseparable from violence, there comes the sacred: there is no lamb without its blood.

None of this *proves* anything, either the 'need' for religion (as if that were a single thing!) or its 'truth'. It suggests only that man is not only, as Aristotle said, a 'political animal' (one which tends to congregate in cities), but also a danger-loving, danger-dreading, God-ridden, blood-soaked creature (Burkert's *Homo Necans*) whose language – and hence whose world – cannot now be purged of the concept of divinity. The evidence for God is indistinguishable from the evidence for language. Can Chomsky's argument that man is a naturally language-forming creature, which seems much less difficult to understand now that we are more familiar with genetic programming, be extended to include the notion that not only sentence-structure but also concept-construction is inherent in us? If this is so, it does not in the least advance the traditional argument that 'God exists', but it does show how difficult, if not impossible, it is for men to convince themselves that He does not.

What I have said here may seem evasive (it is not; it is duplicitous, which is something else). I have been urged to give some account of what it means to me to be a 'secular Jew', as if this were some kind of a refined, or etiolated, version of a full-blooded Jew. What it means to be a Jew, especially in the twentieth century, cannot be covered by an account of personal beliefs, nor am I convinced that anything useful is said about religion by reducing it to a matter of psychological states or needs. On the other hand, I cannot attach much sense to a notion of 'religion' without specificities of a kind which require metaphysical credulity. The case of Judaism, which is more a system of laws than of 'beliefs', differs markedly from that of its *frère-ennemi*, Christianity, whose universalizing affectations have been remarkably serviceable in the advance of a system not always magnanimous in its aggressive piety. However, to be an *un*secular Jew, in a pluralist society like England or the United States, requires intellectual subservience and social exclusivities, not to mention dietary fastidiousness which, had it not been for Hitler, few of us would be disposed to observe. Those who deplore assimilation seem never to notice that to adopt the habits of, for instance, Eastern European Jews, in order somehow to will away the horrors of the Holocaust, is also a kind of assimilation, a wilful adoption of postures and attitudes which, for a Jew born in the United States and educated in England, are both alien and absurd. It is no part of a man's contract, or valuable contact, with the past that he should emigrate to its uncongenial and incomprehensible regions.

If I am willing to say – since it would be absurd to deny – that I am a Jew, it is less because I feel myself to belong to a community of beliefs or practices than because 'denial' would either be contemptible or require apostate allegiance to a religion which rendered me no longer a Jew. The Jewishness of – for easy instance – Spinoza, of Wittgenstein, of Raymond Aron, of Italo Svevo, of Freud, of Menuhin, is not in question, but their lives were conducted in a more or less entirely secular and certainly an intellectually and artistically open-minded manner. I do not doubt that good, useful and generous lives can be lived within an orthodox scheme, but there is no evidence that the only valid Jew must be certified by any religious body (or Israeli official). Cardinal Lustiger, the Archbishop of Paris, who says he is *still* a Jew, suggests how far it is possible to go, without (in one's own opinion at least) having left.

A critic is still at liberty to maintain that I am an instance of the kind of man whom St Paul derided as being neither hot nor cold, but then I am the kind of man who might choose to deride St Paul, precisely because he tried to resolve his contradictions by advocating a religion which is itself sublimely confused: *credo quia impossibile* is, to a heathen mind, a curiously frantic boast.

There might be a place for a personal account of my middle-class Anglo-American upbringing, in the safe heart of a century where millions died for the crime of having been born Jews, but I do not think that this is it. It is more useful, I suspect, to assert the necessity of a scepticism which avoids the dogmatic futility of God-denial but which insists on the need to distinguish law from prophets and which, conscious of the limitations – and even the comedy – of a merely reasonable interest in religion, is disinclined to allow metaphysical dogma to infect mundane practice.

Something very simple, and perhaps very English, follows from this: I have no wish to deprive anyone of his or her right to worship God, in whatever form seems good to them, but I believe (if that is the right verb) in the sacredness of the profane, in the necessity of a middle ground of common citizenship in which no unproved and unprovable notion of rectitude – however admirable – gives a warrant for uncivil coercion, still less for social disqualification or religiously sanctioned murder (or mutilation).

Only a fool can fail to recognize the limitations of a secular society, based on a system of interpenetrating uncertainties; only a villain can propose that there is anything better in prospect for so systematically duplicitous a creature as man. The paradox seems to be that scepticism leads to an adaptable and free society, while certainty, however licensed, limits human intelligence, destroys individuality and leads to the ruinous triumph of intolerance.

Bertrand Russell once argued (only once) that if it could be proved that the destruction of the Jews could secure God's promise of heaven on earth, there could be no reasonable argument against it. He was wrong; not even God's promise *necessarily* warrants committing a crime. Still less, it seems to me, does the attribution of the scriptural doctrines of any religion to His personal dictation justify the enactment of cruelty or murder. If I am asked to say who thinks otherwise, I can only invite you to look at the absurd world we live in.

– 4 –

ISLAM AND CIVIL SOCIETY

HRH Crown Prince El Hassan bin Talal is the 42nd generation direct descendant of the Prophet Mohammad. His branch of the Hashemite family ruled in Mecca from 1201 CE to 1925 CE. He has written numerous articles and published three books on political and regional issues. He has initiated several religious interfaith dialogues – primarily with the Orthodox Centre of the Ecumenical Patriarchate (Chambesy), the Pontifical Council for Interreligious Dialogue (Vatican) and the Independent Commission on Christian Muslim Relations (Deanery of Windsor). He plays polo for Jordan and holds a black belt in Taekwondo. He is also a proficient helicopter pilot.

HRH Crown Prince El Hassan Bin Talal
of the Hashemite Kingdom of Jordan

On Diversity
Among his signs are the creation of heaven and earth and the diversity of your tongues and colours. (30: 22)

On Belief
There shall be no compulsion in religion. (2: 256)

On Judgement
Your duty is only to warn them: you are not their keeper. As for those that turn their backs and disbelieve, Allah will inflict on them the supreme chastisement. To Us they shall return, and We will bring them to account. (88: 21–26)

On Coexistence
Do not revile the idols which they invoke besides Allah, lest in their ignorance they should spitefully revile Allah. We have planned the actions of all men. To their Lord they shall return, and He will declare to them all that they have done. (6: 108)

On Discrimination
Now Pharaoh made himself a tyrant in the land. He divided his people into castes, one group of which he persecuted, putting their sons to death and sparing their daughters. Truly, he was an evil-doer. (28: 4)

Based on a lecture to the Charlemagne Institute
LONDON, JUNE 1996

THE WAVE OF democratization unleashed by the end of the cold war has fundamentally transformed the political landscape in every part of the globe. In this year of elections, more people than ever before are casting ballots to determine their own futures. Political participation and public accountability are the watchwords of the decade. However, underpinning this tremendous surge of political change is the phenomenon known as civil society.

In contemporary political philosophy, civil society needs democratic social interaction. It exists outside the boundaries of the family, but lies short of the state. It involves organizing virtually everything that happens between individual citizens and the state that is not violent. Almost any autonomous group or association which comes into existence by the will and efforts of its members may be considered part of civil society. But civil society also requires standards of behaviour. Activity within civil society and tolerance to those with different views is perhaps its keystone.

Civil society thus represents two ideals: the right of each citizen to interact with a representative and accountable government; and the establishment of a set of rules of behaviour between civil society and the state, as well as within civil society itself.

Some scholars believe that civil society is either absent or ineffective in the Muslim world. They claim that Muslim countries, and the Middle East in particular, have no part in the global process of democratization. Those who hold this view usually see Islam as an obstacle to the emergence of participatory and pluralist politics.

They argue that nothing in Islamic tradition resembles the idea of representative government, or the notion of society as composed of various autonomous, self-activating groups and associations. Claiming that autocracy and acquiescence are the dominant traditions of Islamic history, such scholars generally conclude that any present or future Muslim community will almost by definition lack a vibrant civil society and participatory system of government.

However, a growing number of scholars are now questioning this idea that the Muslim world lacks the ability to achieve more inclusive political processes. They point to historical and contemporary evidence to show that both the organization and the standards of behaviour of civil society are present in the Muslim world. Such scholars conclude that there are indeed good prospects for more representative government.

For my part, I believe that this second perspective is much closer to reality. I believe that the Muslim world has always known activities as well as standards of behaviour that are characteristic of civil society; and I believe that the outlook for the future is promising: Of course, Westminster-style democracy has not, as yet, established firm roots throughout the Muslim world. But I would suggest that commentators who reject the possibility of civil society and democratization are overlooking a gradual but nevertheless thoroughgoing process of evolution that is changing our region as comprehensively as any revolution, with perhaps more enduring effects.

To make this case, I will first discuss the Islamic tradition, especially as it relates to the standards of behaviour of civil society. I will then move on to survey some contemporary trends in the Muslim world, especially as they relate to its organization.

Muslims believe that Islam embodies the complete truth about human existence. Those who say that Islam and civil society are incompatible claim that belief systems which profess to be sole custodians of the truth are seldom disposed towards tolerance and pluralism. However, this critique overlooks the fact that an intrinsic part of the Islamic conception of truth is its acknowledgement of and respect for diversity. Indeed, it is this which has allowed Islam to grow and to enrich itself over the centuries by drawing on the deep wellspring of human variety.

Islam holds that differences among human beings are willed by God. The Holy Koran tells us: 'Had your Lord pleased, He would have united all mankind.' (11.118) Human variety is considered to be one of the proofs of God. Muslim tradition holds that diversity, for example of our appearances, languages and so forth, is among his signs. So while Islam conceives of itself as the completion of previous religious traditions, it does not demand sterile uniformity. Rather, it commands that human beings respect and learn from each other's differences. The Holy Koran says: 'O mankind, We have created you from a male and a female and divided you into nations and tribes that you might know one another.' (49:13)

As with other variations, human differences in matters of belief are therefore respected by Islam. It is not for Muslims to force their beliefs on others. Islam does not condone compulsion in religion. The Koran is extremely emphatic in making this point: 'Had your Lord pleased, all the people of the earth would have believed in Him. Would you then force faith upon men?' (10:99) The essential corollary of this position is the far-reaching idea that it is not humanity's place to judge the merits of different beliefs. Muslims are encouraged to engage in discussion and dialogue with non-Muslims, but judgement is the prerogative of God alone.

On the basis of these principles, Islamic tradition enjoins mutual tolerance and coexistence among and between human communities. It also stresses the equality and dignity of each and every human soul. The Prophet Mohammed is reliably reputed to have said: 'All people are equal. They are as equal as the teeth on a comb. There is no claim of merit of an Arab over a non-Arab, or of a white over a black person, or a male over a female. Only God-fearing people merit a preference with God.' Furthermore, the idea that rights of citizenship accrue on the basis of residence was well known to Islam. For example, the Holy Koran rebukes Egypt's Pharaoh for discriminating against the Jewish community in Egypt.

Thus Islamic teaching favours equality; respects individual and communal rights of belief and citizenship; and advocates the peaceful management of diversity. Although there are of course examples of behaviour to the contrary, they are the exceptions, for the historical record shows that Muslim societies have in the main practised these principles.

The earliest illustration of these principles in practice is a document known as the Constitution of Medina, which articulated the agreements concluded between the prophet Mohammed and the non-Muslim tribes of Medina. The Constitution enabled each party to keep its own laws and customs. It conferred rights and obligations of citizenship among members of the community on the basis of residence and religious belief. The Constitution of Medina is thus at base a civil code, and a blueprint for Islamic pluralism.

In later times, the *millet* system granted non-Muslims a clear bill of rights, and empowered them to run their own communal affairs. Under this system, non-Muslim communities paid a poll tax in return for exemption from the obligation of *jihad*. They were eligible for all but the very highest executive positions. In every other respect, they had the same worldly rights and obligations as Muslims. These norms can be seen as a solid basis for civil society in the Muslim world. However, there are also many organizational precedents in Muslim history which should be considered.

Traditional Muslim society was ordered around a central political authority, combining temporal and spiritual affairs; but public space was immediately shared by a variety of collective associations. These included the merchants, guilds, *ulama*,

Muslim and non-Muslim sects, and tribes. Some of these groupings enjoyed considerable autonomy from central government in terms of power as well as resources. They ran most of their own internal affairs through elected or appointed leaders, elders and notables, known as *Ahlu al-Hal wa al-akd*, or the Solvers and Binders. It was their responsibility to manage intra-communal affairs and inter-communal conflicts. They represented the interests of the people in general and their own constituencies in particular to the central authority, while conveying and legitimizing central authority's decisions to their constituencies. Central authority collected taxes, administered justice, and maintained public order and defence. However, it was not expected to provide social services or to exercise direct economic functions. These were mostly left to local communities, which were grouped according to primordial, religious, ethnic and occupational solidarities. Thus traditional Muslim societies relied on communal formations for many of their political and economic needs, as well as for identity.

It should also be recalled that trade was central to Muslim society, and that various civil society mechanisms evolved to facilitate it. The Middle East has the longest recorded history of civil and private law regarding the rights and property of the trader. The contractual forms in which such rights are expressed were probably also pioneered in the region. Although interest-based groups such as trade associations may have originated elsewhere, they rose to prominence in the medieval Muslim world. Just like their successor organizations of the present day, such as the Chambers of Commerce, they enjoyed considerable success in lobbying central authority on behalf of their members' interests, whether or not those interests coincided with the policy goals of the government.

This brings me to the present-day Muslim world, and the question of whether credible and accessible mechanisms exist for citizens and communities to organize themselves according to their interests and to address their views to government.

As one might expect from the religious and historical background which I have outlined, a wide variety of interest-based groups does exist in today's Muslim world. Although they seldom receive attention in the West, countless political parties, religious groups, press organs, professional associations and trade unions function outside the government in virtually every Muslim country. Innumerable voluntary organizations, human rights bodies, women's associations, minority rights groups and social organizations are to be found throughout the region. Citizens are constantly meeting, both formally and informally, to discuss the issues that concern them – ranging from local health and education to national economic and foreign policy – and to organize ways in which to put their views to the government. Some governments welcome such activity; some do not. In both cases, however, it continues and it cannot be stopped.

The case in Jordan provides an example. We are committed to the process of democratization and political inclusion, and we welcome the activities of civil society organizations. Our citizens have been gradually brought into the political process through direct parliamentary and local elections as well as through civil society. Organizations such as trade unions, religious institutions, community development groups, charitable bodies and clubs of all sorts function freely in Jordan, expressing their views and lobbying for the interests of their members.

In Jordan, civil society forms the culture within which an ongoing national dialogue on state policy takes place; while the state is helping civil society to mature by ensuring fair play for all. It remains the ultimate guarantor of the rule of law and the constitutional rights of every citizen. While the state does not condone the activities of groups whose goal is to overthrow the political system, it fully supports those who wish to work within the Constitution. Thus all political parties in Jordan must respect each other's right to exist, and must abide by the norms of mutual tolerance and equal participation spelled out in the Constitution and the National Charter. We believe that without such state guarantees of fair play, democratization would disintegrate into chaos. But the existence of a vibrant civil society, both in terms of traditional formations such as the tribe, and in terms of more modern groups such as the professional associations, can only enhance the process. Many commentators now suggest that the existence of Jordanian civil society, together with the prevailing spirit of tolerance and coexistence, have played a major part in Jordan's remarkable record of stability over the years.

The conclusion is clear. At the grass-roots of Muslim culture, civil society organizations are thriving. Democratization and transparent accountable governmental practices are beginning to take hold. I believe that the prospects for the future are indeed promising. I say this not only on the basis of Jordan's experience, but also on the basis of studies that are coming out of Turkey, North Africa, the Arabian Gulf, Indonesia, Malaysia and so forth. The immense range of civil society organizations that emerges from such studies proves that Muslim citizens are willing and able to play a direct role in shaping the policies that govern their lives. Islam is not an obstacle to reform. On the contrary, Islamic teaching and tradition provide solid bases for the development of civil society. Civility and citizenship, tolerance and pluralism are fundamental to Islamic tradition. These perspectives are increasingly being articulated by Muslim thinkers who are drawing on the best of this tradition to develop moderate and progressive interpretations of Islam.

However, these vital developments appear to have little impact on the global image of contemporary Islam. Perceptions of the Muslim world are distorted beyond recognition. The general contempt that the Western media often display towards Islam exacerbates the situation. While images of Muslim religious extremism are burned into Western consciousness, they are by no means universally accepted in the Muslim world as models of piety. Yet alternative models of Islamic leadership, which pursue a path of tolerance, pluralism and moderation, are not widely known in the West.

It should be acknowledged that some figures from the Muslim world have tried to initiate a global dialogue at various levels. For my part, I have been involved in inter-cultural and inter-faith initiatives for many years, and have always sought to put forward the moderate Muslim perspective. However, it is regrettable that such initiatives never receive the kind of media coverage that violent acts receive. One cannot help but feel a sense of frustration, for much depends on the success of such initiatives; and their success depends largely on their public recognition.

– 5 –
THE MEDIA AS DEMON IN THE POST-MODERNIST AGE OF SECULARISM[1]

Professor Akbar Ahmed is a distinguished anthropologist, writer and commentator on Islamic affairs. He is a Fellow of Selwyn College, Cambridge. He is author of several books including *Discovering Islam: Making Sense of Muslim History and Society* (1988) which inspired the television series *Living Islam* for which he was the chief consultant. He has also written numerous articles for journals and newspapers. He is currently producing a feature film and writing a book on Mr Jinnah, the founder of Pakistan.

PROFESSOR AKBAR S. AHMED

TWO CHEERS FOR SECULARISM

When Saddam Hussein invaded Kuwait in the summer of 1990 he killed more than Kuwaiti independence. He also shattered the complacency of those who were dreaming of a stable and harmonious post-cold-war new world order for the 1990s which would set the stanchions in place for the political architecture of the 21st century. Within days George Bush and Mrs Thatcher were calling him Hitler; many Arabs, on the other hand, saw him as a champion and compared him to Nasser, even Saladin; Iraqis, hedging their bets, added the name of the pre-Islamic King of Babylon, Nebuchadnezzar.

Young soldiers deep in America, at one end of the world and in rural Pakistan, at the other, began to pack for duty on the Arabian peninsula; Americans, who provide aid to Pakistan, had made an offer which Pakistanis could not refuse and therefore they agreed to supply troops to fight alongside the Americans. Young Stuart Lockwood, one of the hostages in Baghdad, had his head patted by Saddam on television and instantly became part of history. Muslims everywhere protested at the presence of non-Muslim troops in the land of Makkah and Medinah. Arabs accused the Americans of being like Rambo. Palestinians, taking heart from Saddam's support, renewed the *intifada* and their deaths in Jerusalem provoked talk of *jihad*, the holy war, among Arabs; Israel, threatened by Saddam, once again evoked the spirit of Masada, the ancient garrison besieged by the Romans. The war that followed had about it the inevitability of Greek tragedy.

In the future, major international crises would follow this pattern, which was characterized by several features: first, the involvement of the media. The media were everywhere. Every gesture and every word of the main players like Saddam were news, to be discussed and analysed. Second, the inter-connection of the world was made apparent whether people – our example of American and Pakistani soldiers – or economies: not only oil supplies to the West but the remittances of the South Asian workers were affected. Third, a feeling, a mood, grew, fed by the earlier points, that henceforth a crisis of this nature could escalate uncontrollably to a world disaster. A global perception therefore formed, not unanimous on cause and effect, but one that reflected concern for the interdependence of life on earth.

Most of this was new and frightening, but there was an eerie element of *déjà vu* in the drama, as if half-awake we had seen some of it before. Over the past two years another crisis had been simmering. In it we had heard the principles of freedom of expression being defended – Voltaire was often cited – against those Muslims who felt their religious beliefs were outraged by *The Satanic Verses*. The age of secularism – as represented by the Western media – discovered just how sensitive Muslims were about Islam.

Muslims believed the Prophet and his family were insulted and the authenticity

---

1   The author expresses his gratitude to Routledge for allowing him to use material from his book *Postmodernism and Islam: Predicament and Promise*, 1992, for this chapter.

of the Qu'rān challenged. Ayatollah Khomeini elevated the Muslim response into an international affair by issuing a *fatwa*, a declaration, condemning the author, Salman Rushdie, to death; then, by dying, he left the issue suspended in mid-air to eternity; no Iranian could revoke or cancel it.

Shortly after the Gulf war, to Muslims it appeared that yet another strand was woven into the rope being used to bind Islam: the story of the Pakistani and Arab bank, the BCCI, broke. Here was massive fraud, corruption, cooking of books, drugs, big names; these businessmen would bring a blush of shame to the cheeks of J.R. Ewing. The media went wild with glee at what was one of the biggest banking scandals in history; the fact that most of the key players were Muslim added to the pleasure of the chase. The entire globe seemed to have been drawn into the scandal. Links were established to Abu Nidal on the one hand and Pakistan's nuclear programme on the other. It became the Bank of Cocaine and Crooks in the Western media. In 1991 the Western media were freely placing Muslims in the context of what they labelled a 'criminal' culture. Religion, the argument set in an age dominated by secularism implied, was inherently flawed.

Ordinary, everyday, average Muslims may not agree with the *fatwa*, they may despise the military dictator in Iraq, they may loathe the fraud and corruption at the bank, but they also resent the cavalier way in which they are treated by association in the media. They are still anxious to point out that the reality in each case is more complex than meets the eye; they will not have liked Rushdie's book, they will be vicariously thrilled that Saddam stood up to the West and spoke up for the Palestinians, even that the BCCI may be the target of Western wrath because it is the first major international Muslim bank.

There is no way an ordinary Muslim can make his views known in the media which floods hostile words and images over and around him. He is portrayed as a fanatic over the book, politically unstable through the dictator and corrupt by the actions of the bank. In the end, unable to convey his arguments, helpless and impotent, he is as cynical of Western motives as those of the military dictator and the corrupt bankers – they are all the same, he will say. But he is also as disgusted as he is confused with his own sense of impotence in shaping reality around him; he can no longer challenge what is real or unreal, no longer separate reality from the illusion of the media.

We note that Islam is the common factor intertwining most of the people mentioned above and ask: is Islam to be isolated in the coming time as a force for anarchy and disorder? Islam from the time of the Crusades was seen as barbarous, licentious, the enemy of Christianity – in our age, in addition, it is seen as anarchic, minatory, monolithic. The Islamic peril is now the greatest threat to the West besides which the Red and Yellow perils pale into insignificance.

Raising Questions

These contemporary crises were different yet in some ways similar; they forced us to ask questions, to challenge common assumptions, to look at the familiar in a different light. The kinetic energy which was created in turn sparked ideas and prejudices, controversy and argument. The crossing of cultural boundaries created the misinterpretation of foreign idiom causing great offence and agitation, great misunderstanding, on all sides. The crises brought together a bewildering collage of historical and popular images that, through communications technology, bonded the entire globe. The audio-visual media allowed, as never before in history, an instant access to news, an unsettling, dazzling, juxtaposition of diverse pictures, a variety of discourses. High philosophy and comic book ideas, historical facts and pop sociology jostled and mingled. All this was made possible by other recent developments such as mass transport, the electronic and printing media and the development of the global economy.

It was the media that juxtaposed for us images of people like Hitler and Saddam, Bush and Lockwood, Rambo and the Pakistani soldier, Saladin and Nebuchadnezzar, Khomeini and Rushdie, Voltaire and the Prophet, the Pope and Madonna, and places like Masada and Makkah, Babylon and Jerusalem. The Rushdie affair, the Madonna crisis, the manner of the Gulf confrontation were harbingers of things to come – not peripheral but central to our understanding; the exploration of this theme will be my concern. It is the times and age we live in.

We are living in a period of dramatic change; structures that have held for generations are being pulled down. Changing, too, are notions of the self and of the other, of class, of ethnicity and of nation, although the nature and depth of these are still debatable. A perception is forming that we may be entering a distinct phase of human history, one following modernism and therefore tentatively called post-modernist. However the rupture with the previous period is not complete. For if recent events in the Soviet Union, East Europe and South Africa signify post-modernist impulses, those in Tiananmen Square, the coup which almost ousted Gorbachev in August 1991, and the *fatwa* against Salman Rushdie suggest the strength of tradition and authority. A host of questions, many of them urgent for the approaching time, are thus thrown up for our consideration:

Is there truth in the widely held assumption in the West that after the collapse of communism the next enemy is Islam? What does the 'new world order' we hear so much about mean for Muslims? Is the post-modernist age intrinsically hostile to Islam? Will the strong forces of secularism succeed in obliterating Islam?

Why do the media commentators, whether academics or journalists, so consistently and unanimously disparage Islam? And is the Muslim response, rejecting the Western media as biased, an effective one? If so, how long can they isolate themselves from the global civilization? Will the lampooning and vilification divert Muslims from the values of a religion that advocates compassion and balance? And where are these virtues, so much emphasized in the Qu'rān, to be located in the present Islamic turbulence? Are the so-called moderates 'out' and the so-called extremists 'in' as a consequence of this turbulence?

What intellectual and cultural changes are taking place among Muslims? Is the mosque in danger of being replaced by the mall as the focus of Muslim social and community activity? What does the sermon in the mosque tell us? What does Islam have to say about the 'green' movement and the ecology? How can Muslims retain their central Islamic features – family life, care for children, respect for elders, concepts of modesty etc. – in the face of the contrary philosophy of the post-modernist age? And how can they successfully convey the relevance of their beliefs and customs, their 'message', to the world community of which they are part?

We also go back to the past by asking: How does a religious civilization like Islam, which relies on a defined code of behaviour and traditions based on a holy book, cope in an age which self-consciously puts aside the past and exults in diversity? (The question is relevant to other religious cultures of Semitic origin). How does it relate to the other major Semitic religions? What does it make of the influential civilization of Europe formed by the Greeks? How does European imperialism continue to affect Muslim culture and thinking?

These are important questions and need to be asked of our age. There are many theories in circulation, many processes afoot and many explanations at work.[2] Faith versus scepticism, tradition versus iconoclasm, purity versus eclecticism – it is difficult to relate Islamic post-modernism to Western post-modernism in any coherent or direct manner, or even to establish a causal relationship between the two. Although Muslims may employ some of the conceptual tools of Francois Lyotard or Jean Baudrillard for analysis there must be a parting of company on certain crucial points. While Muslims appreciate the spirit of tolerance, optimism and the drive for self-knowledge in post-modernism they also recognize the threat it poses them with its cynicism and irony. This is a challenge to the faith and piety which lie at the core of their world-view.

In the end, Islamic and Western post-modernism may have little more in common than that they are coetaneous, running concurrently. What we can state is that they may be entering this particular phase of their respective histories through different gates, propelled by different causes, still unsure of certain features, like the nature of the media and formulation of their responses to it, and even with a different understanding of the very nature of the age.

---

2 I point to some in my books *Postmodernism and Islam*, 1992, and *Living Islam*, 1993; *see also* Ahmed and Donnan, *Islam, Globalisation and Postmodernity* (Routledge, 1994).

Muslim Modernism

Let us first clarify what we mean by modernism. We, too, rely on the meaning provided by the Oxford Dictionary. For Muslims then the definition applies to a wide range of activity from Islamic thought to political action, from architecture to modes of dress. But there is a caveat to note.

The Muslim modernist phase was engendered by European colonialism. While more conservative Muslims would have no truck with Europeans – indeed many resisting them through armed struggle – the modernists wished to come to terms with, even incorporate, elements of their civilization. Most sought synthesis and ideally looked for harmony between their own position and that of the Europeans.

One of the earliest and most influential modernist figures is Sir Sayyed Ahmed Khan who lived in India in the last century. The college he established in 1875 in Aligarh, near Delhi, laid the foundations for what was to become a symbol of Muslim identity and lead to the Pakistan movement. The name of his institution, The Muhammadan Anglo-Oriental College, its conscious attempt to emulate Oxbridge, the title of his book, *An Account of The Loyal Muhammadans of India* (1860) and his knighthood, in recognition of his services to the British, convey the essence of this modernist Muslim. The college – later university – was a rich source of recruitment for two other Indian modernist leaders, Muhammad Ali Jinnah and Muhammad Iqbal, who would go on to create Pakistan. Jinnah, too, consciously looked to London, where he was educated, for ideas on politics; Iqbal who studied in Cambridge, cites European writers frequently in his work. Jinnah with his cigar, monocle, Savile Row suits and talk of Westminster-style democracy – in a clipped English accent – is the modernist Muslim leader *par excellence*.

All this served a purpose. Modernism provided important weapons to Muslims like Sir Sayyed, Iqbal and Jinnah. Through their understanding of British ways and ideas they could engage successfully with the colonial power. These Muslims would turn the skills they had acquired from the British against them to best represent the interests of their community.

Muhammad Abduh, the father of Arab modernism and rector of Al-Azhar, and his disciple Rashid Rida, early this century, are the influential Arab modernists. Both were inspired by the late 19th-century figure of Jamalaldin Afghani. Afghani's sympathetic interaction with European intellectuals on the one hand and advocacy of pan-Islamism on the other make him a central figure in Muslim modernism.

Across the Muslim world – Ataturk in Turkey, Amanullah in Afghanistan, the Shah in Iran (both father and son), Jinnah in Pakistan – leaders looked to the West for inspiration in moulding their societies and projecting modernity. Their actions expressed their position: Ataturk ordering the shaving of beards as symbolic of tradition, Amanullah encouraging the removal of the veils that women wore, the Shah suppressing the clergy and Jinnah rebuking admirers for calling him a

'Maulana', a religious leader.

In turn, the more orthodox would oppose these leaders. The pressure of the Muslim Brotherhood would be felt by Nasser; Sadat would lose his life to them. Jinnah, for many Muslims was the 'Quaid-i-Azam' or the great leader, for others he was 'Kafiri-Azam' or the great *kafir*, non-believer. The Shah of Iran became the symbol of a *kafir* for the Islamic revolution. The oscillation continues in Muslim society and explains an important dynamic of it.

Muslim leaders even after independence would continue to interact with, and borrow from, the legacy of modern ideas they acquired in the British institutions which had helped shape them: the London law colleges (Jinnah), Sandhurst (Field Marshal Ayub Khan of Pakistan), Harrow (King Hussein of Jordan and agnates), Oxbridge (Mr Bhutto and his daughter, Benazir Bhutto) or indigenous but British-style institutions (Nasser). There was almost a distinctly British code of behaviour in their attitude to their main opponents: Jinnah admitting that Indian Muslims had lost their greatest friend on hearing the news that his archrival, Gandhi, was shot dead; Nasser, after his military coup, allowing King Farouk to escape to the south of France in the royal yacht; Ayub, after his coup, permitting Iskander Mirza to proceed to London; Bhutto, after coming to power, leaving Ayub to spend his last years in his own home as a free citizen and not even bringing him to court on corruption charges as demanded by his party. This would change later. The Shah of Iran would be hounded to his death by the Ayatollahs and Bhutto himself hung in jail like a common criminal because General Zia would not pardon him.

Modern was translated by Muslim leaders as a drive to acquire Western education, technology and industry. Ideas of democracy and representative government were also discussed although with reservation on the part of the élite. For those who looked to the communist countries and Moscow for assistance, modernism also meant the imported ideas of secularism, socialism and state-controlled industrialization. In the 1960s economists and advisers from the two superpowers laid down the golden rules for modern progress, whether the Harvard economists in Pakistan or the Moscow planners in Cairo. Strong treaties or security pacts bound many Muslim countries to one or other of the superpowers: Ayub's Pakistan through CENTO and SEATO with the USA, Nasser's Egypt with the USSR. Prestigious central projects – Nasser's Aswan Dam, Ayub's capital, Islamabad – became symbols of national pride; the country's planners became the wise men behind the five-year economic plans which incorporated all aspects of life from health, to industry, to education; the government became the standard-bearer of modernity. The central issue was, as the Oxford Dictionary told us, to subordinate religious belief to harmony with modern thought. There was thus a mimetic quality about Muslim modernism. Sometimes these leaders spoke out against the West but tell-tale signs gave them away. Their Western suits, for example, suggested they remained in thrall.

If modern meant the pursuit of Western education, technology and industrialization in the first flush of the post-colonial period, post-modern would mean a reversion to traditional Muslim values and a rejection of modernism. This would generate an entire range of Muslim responses from politics to clothes to architecture.

For us the definition is literal: it is the period following that of modernism. With an important caveat or two we therefore accept the use of the term post-modern. We emphasize its European context and origin; and we point out that many of the features of modernism are continued although in an altered form, in post-modernism. The application of the term thus assists us in better understanding the contemporaneous phase of Muslim history. In Muslim society post-modernism means a shift to ethnic or Islamic identity (not necessarily the same thing and at times opposed to each other) as against an imported foreign or Western one, a rejection of modernity, the emergence of a young, faceless, discontented leadership, cultural schizophrenia, a sense of entering an apocalyptic moment in history and above all, a numbing awareness of the power and pervasive nature of the Western media which are perceived as hostile.

Discussions of post-modernism in the West relate it to an intellectual period with specific cultural characteristics and intellectual content. Secularism is a main characteristic of Western post-modernism as it manifests itself in the media. Writers are easily labelled: James Joyce is recognizably modern and Jean Baudrillard is post-modern. In the Muslim world there is a different emphasis, different markers, different understanding. Muslims would link the post-modernist phase to the political history of their nations. If post-modernism in the West was fostered by a milieu which encouraged the growing security and confidence after the Second World War, opposite forces were at work among Muslims. The catalyst may well have been provided by the political and military disasters after the first flush of independence from the colonial powers (although not all Muslim countries were formally colonized).

The defeat and humiliation of the Arabs in 1967 at the hands of Israel and the loss of territory – east Jerusalem, the West Bank, Gaza and the Golan Heights – was followed shortly by the victory of India over Pakistan in 1971 which resulted in the loss of the majority province for Pakistan. Although in the Pakistan case the Army was used to suppress the Bangladesh freedom movement and therefore drew widespread criticism, the spectacle of a hundred thousand Muslim soldiers languishing in Indian prison camps was not an edifying one for most Pakistanis. These events did not have a recent precedent and were seen by Muslims to reflect the bankruptcy of their secular or modern rulers. Muslim humiliation was deep; morale was at its nadir.

The modern period had led Muslims into a cul-de-sac. Dictators, coups, corruption and nepotism in politics, low education standards, the intellectual paresis, the continuing oppression of women and the under-privileged and grossly unequal distribution of wealth were some of its characteristics. The multinational companies and their visible impact in creating what was seen as a corrupt local élite, the large scale migration from the rural to the urban areas and consequent social disruption in traditional life and the failure to build effective institutions of the modern State were other characteristics. Muslims were coming to the same conclusion as Anthony Giddens who in *The Consequences of Modernity*[3] saw modernity as 'a Western project'.

The reality of Muslim life was a far cry from the edifying and noble Islamic ideal (for a discussion of the ideal type, which is based primarily in the Qu'rān and life of the Prophet *see* Ahmed 1988).[4] Muslims, as most people who believe in God do, asked, if God had abandoned them. Other Muslims turned the question round: had they abandoned God? The answer pointed in the direction of Islam and they turned to God (in troubled times this is a common theme in Muslim history).[5]

Islamic Resurgence

The decade of the 1970s for Muslims began and was sustained with unparalleled Muslim activity: the Ramadan war in 1973, the Arab oil embargo in the same year led by the vigorously dedicated King Faisal, General Zia's assumption of power in 1977 and his Islamization programme, the start of the Afghan *jihad*, holy war, to liberate Afghanistan in 1979, the bloody and violent attempt, also in the same year, by Juhaiman and his group to seize the Kaaba in Makkah – for Muslims the holiest of the holy, the action sent shock-waves wherever they lived; and finally, the culmination of the decade with the coming to power of Ayatollah Khomeini at the head of the Islamic revolution in Iran, in 1979. Islamic activity was also noted in countries far from the Middle East like Nigeria and Indonesia. At all levels the Muslim leaders mentioned above consciously evoked tradition, whether in the rhetoric and idiom of politics, observing the fast during the month of Ramadan or wearing traditional dress, in particular avoiding the tie as a symbol of Western dress.[6]

Let us take the Ramadan war, which set the tone for the coming years. While the earlier wars with Israel were seen in terms of Arab nationalism and socialism, the Ramadan war was dense with Islamic symbols and rhetoric. The war was named 'Ramadan' after the sacred month of fasting during which it occurred; its code name was Badr, the first major victory for Islam led by the Prophet himself; those who died were not regarded as patriots but as *shaheed*, religious martyrs; and the

3   Giddens, Anthony, *The Consequences of Modernity* (Polity Press, 1990).
4   Ahmed, *Discovering Islam* (Routledge, 1988).
5   Ibid., chapter 3, section 6.
6   *See* Ahmed, *Living Islam* (BBC Books, 1993).

battle-cry was *Allah-u-Akbar*, God is most great, the traditional call for prayer. (Almost twenty years later Saddam, the erstwhile socialist, would follow some of these steps during the Gulf crisis including the stitching of *Allah-u-Akbar* onto the Iraqi flag.)

One of the key players in the Islamic revival was King Faisal. He first hastened the end of the Nasser era among Arabs by challenging Nasser's leadership. He then provided a vigorous Islamic direction to the Arabs and indeed the Muslim world. The first meeting of the Islamic heads of state in Rabat in 1969 was a personal triumph for him. The Islamic Conference Organization was formed with its headquarters in Jeddah. By helping to organize a similar meeting in Lahore, Pakistan, he was drawing non-Arab Muslims into the Middle East arena. Faisal's use of oil prices as a weapon in the 1970s also proved effective as it underlined the link with the region of those nations who needed oil. The millions of Muslims who were employed on the Arabian peninsula, especially from South Asia – like the three million Pakistanis – provided further leverage.

But Muslim activity was not confined to battlefields and diplomatic conferences. A period of intellectual effervescence had begun. The first world conference on Muslim education was held in Makkah in 1977 which generated a series of academic papers, books and conferences. Another equally autotrophic international attempt towards an 'Islamization of Knowledge' was made by scholars like Ismail al-Faruqi in the 1980s which challenged many existing modernist ideas. Muslim educationists, like Ali Ashraf, laboured to create an 'Islamic education' (1979, 1985), economists, like Khurshid Ahmad, 'Islamic economics' (1981), and like Siddiqui, 'Islamic banking' (1983), sociologists, like Ba-Yunus, an 'Islamic sociology' (1985) and anthropologists an 'Islamic anthropology' (Ahmed 1986).[7] Books like Edward Said's *Orientalism* (1978) which forcefully argued that the West could know Islam only in an exploitative, hostile way, further provided ideas fuelling the challenge to Western scholarship. Muslim radical scholars carried this argument to its logical conclusion, rejecting everything from the West out of hand and thereby set the pace, if not the agenda, for Muslim scholarship.

In our times the one picture which perhaps best symbolizes a similar clash between the West and Islam is the burning of Rushdie's book: it is the contemporary equivalent of the 19th-century charge. This time Muslims, once again convinced that they are protesting an attack on their beliefs, shouting *Allah-u-Akbar*, at demonstrations endorsed by their elders, march towards the waiting media. Once again the most advanced Western technology meets Muslim faith, once again it is a massacre, this time of the Muslim image in the West. We witness again two mutually uncomprehending systems colliding: monumental contempt and arrogance on one side, blind faith and fury on the other.

---

7 For an overview *see* chapter ten, 'The reconstruction of Muslim thought', in Ahmed, *Discovering Islam* op. cit.

It is the nature of this complex historical encounter, exacerbated with each incident, which feeds into the Muslim incapacity to respond coolly and meaningfully. Muslims being killed on the West Bank or in Kashmir, their mosques being threatened with demolition in Jerusalem or in Ayodhya, India, are seen throughout the Muslim world on television and cause instant dismay and anger. The threat to the mosques has deep resonances in Muslim history. The one in Jerusalem is called after Umar, one of the greatest Muslims and rulers after the Prophet, the one in India after Babar, the founder of the Mughal dynasty. One is over a millennium in age, the other almost half a millennium. It is a milieu of distrust and violence within which Muslims see their lives enmeshed. The recent killings of Muslims by Muslims across the world – a Vice Chancellor in Kashmir, an Imam in Belgium, an aged writer in Turkey – is one response. It demonstrates the attempt to force greater commitment on the community, to push people off the fence, to obliterate the moderate and reasonable position; it also demonstrates desperation.

Taming the Demon
Stephen Hawking sums up his views on the secrets of the universe in the last lines of his book, *A Brief History of Time*, thus:

> However, if we do discover a complete theory, it should in time be understandable in broad principle by every one, not just a few scientists. Then we shall all, philosophers, scientists, and just ordinary people, be able to take part in the discussion of the question of why it is that we and the universe exist. If we find the answer to that, it would be the ultimate triumph of human reason – for then we would know the mind of God.[8]

Even for a scientist it is not possible to squeeze God out of existence. Einstein had already hinted at this: 'Science without religion is lame, religion without science is blind'. That is why I find Hawking's book on the universe full of spiritual content, dense with hints of a divine presence; that is perhaps why it remained so long on the bestseller list. He wasn't a scientist expelling God from the universe. He was a searcher pointing to clues that God was to be found somewhere underneath the scientific formulae and jargon. Hawking breaches the thin line between science and religion and illustrates for us the various paths that lead to God.

We attribute many things to poor Marx. His idea of God being dead is one. But the idea of God dead, or of never ever having existed at all, is not a recent one. From the start of history human beings have been plagued by such doubts; 'Who am I?' 'Does my life have meaning?' 'Is there a higher – divine being up there in the skies?' 'If so, how can I know for sure?' Indeed even the prophets from time to time sought to reaffirm their faith, to purify their ideas, to seek clarification; they retreated alone to caves, wandered in deserts, fasted or kept long silences hoping this would assist in the discovery of answers.

8 Hawking, Stephen, *A Brief History of Time* (Bantam Press, 1988) p. 175.

Neither silence nor escape is an easy task in our times. What the post-modernist age offers us by its very definition is the potential, the possibility, the vision of harmony through understanding. In theory, in posture, even by the logic of its provenance, post-modernism suggests tolerance and *laissez-faire*. To each his own thing. This is not so in practice. In their shrill intolerance of opposing voices, some of those labelled 'post-modernist' authors sound suspiciously like other more conventional authors of earlier times. We saw how lines were crossed in the Rushdie affair at many points, stereotypes negated and paradoxes created. Many staunch Christian priests were vocally supportive of Muslims while many liberal intellectuals sounded like Inquisition priests in their shrill and blanket condemnations. In the one case, a millennium of hostility to Muslims was set aside, in the other a century of the liberal philosophy.

In their emphasis on ethnicity, many post-modernist political movements generate racial violence which is as barbaric as any we know of from primeval tribal warfare. Ethnicity is the unprimed and potentially most explosive reality of human society, as we saw in East Europe and the USSR. Its links with post-modernism are still to be discovered clearly. Muslims and Marxists slit the throats of fellow Muslims and fellow Marxists. Ethnicity in these cases overrides larger ideological loyalties. Our age is littered with notoriously famous examples.

In the coming time there will be major battles in many theatres. One will be between the forces of openness, rationality, equilibrium, balance on the one hand and malevolence and prejudice on the other. The one will stand for tolerance, understanding and harmony, the other will preach hatred, intolerance and disharmony; and in that line-up it is not altogether clear who stands where. Strange and unexpected allies will form reflecting interesting points of contact.

The divisions between Islam versus the West, the Orient versus the Occident, North versus South no longer work. During the Gulf war in 1991 possibly the most sensitive and consistent anti-war writing came from Edward Pearce, John Pilger and Martin Woollacott. In spite of their obvious loathing for military dictators they pointed out the devastating consequences of that kind of war for the ordinary Iraqi.

One kind of Muslim and Jew, Christian and agnostic will face another kind of their own compatriot in the future. The preparation for that battle is already beginning to take place. An important shot was fired by the unique conference held in Oslo to discuss 'The Anatomy of Hate' in the summer of 1990. The names of the participants read like a roll-call of the most inspiring figures of the late 20th century such as Nelson Mandela and Vaclav Havel. But it was also noted that Muslims were conspicuous by their absence; once again Muslims seemed to be out of step with the world.

This was not so in another event, equally unique and equally illustrative of the nature of our age, although different in style and content from the one in Oslo, which took place in London in September 1991. It was the charity dinner organized by Imran Khan for the first cancer hospital in Pakistan. Assembled were six hundred guests including international celebrities like Mick Jagger, Jerry Hall and Vinod Khanna, the Indian film star who had flown in for the evening from Bombay. Dinner ended with a *qawali* sung by Nusrat Fateh Ali and his group, fresh from their triumph on British TV. As I had a vantage point on the high table I was able to observe the impact of the *qawali* on the guests.

Nusrat and his group, sitting cross-legged, made themselves comfortable on the dais opposite the High Table. Like all *qawalis* it began with the *hamd* in praise of God. Many of the Muslims were soon in ecstasy at the power of the *hamd. Allah hu, Allah hu, Allah hu* – Oh God, Oh God, Oh God – chanted Nusrat's group, finding an echo in the spellbound audience. I watched Mick Jagger. Seated on the High Table, opposite the *qawali* group, he was shaking his head and shoulders in rhythm – and I thought: to hear the *hamd* in London before such a large and enthusiastic audience and to see Mick Jagger among them shaking to *Allah hu* was only possible in our age. Here was contradiction, here was juxtaposition and here was hope; somewhere in the midst of the emotions and ideas flowing about in the hall diverse points were meeting in harmony. Truly, as Nusrat sang, God is great.

In any case rigid boundaries are no longer easy to maintain. A person can – and does – possess overlapping identities; in our age this allows the possibility of enrichment and pleasure. A person can be a devout Muslim and a loyal citizen of Britain. Multiple identities mean eclecticism, which requires tolerance of others. Without some conscious attempt to comprehend the logic of this formula, we reduce it to a meaningless shibboleth.

The 'catastrophe' theory, which links every event, however insignificant, to a chain that includes all of us everywhere in the world, no longer appears far-fetched. A leaf falling in India is heard in Canada, a fridge switched on in China causes dismay in Britain. Until a few years ago the USA could occupy Vietnam, the USSR march into Hungary, the Israelis crush the Palestinians and little could be done about it by the rest of the world; indeed little was known. Only the secret services talked darkly of covert operations and politicians used elegant but empty phrases. But with the Iraqi invasion of Kuwait and the war which followed, the world was suddenly faced with the prospect of a major world conflict involving in some degree virtually every major power and, above all, involving us all in some way. All the worst aspects of modern war – chemical weapons, nuclear strikes, hostage killing – loomed before us.

The world is so shrunk, so inter-linked and so claustrophobic that the Iraqi action once and for all dispelled the euphoria that resulted in the West after the collapse of communism and the prospects of world peace. From now on one man with a bomb in his briefcase and a wild dream can hold the world to ransom; his ignorance of the number and kinds of boundaries violated will not matter. Ours is, therefore, not a simple world.

There will be, increasingly, little elbow room, limited space, on our planet; this is because of the nature of the post-modernist era. The West, through the dominant global civilization, will continue to expand its boundaries to encompass the world; traditional civilizations will resist in some areas, accommodate to change in others. In the main, only one, Islam, will stand firm in its path. Islam, therefore, appears to be set on a collision course with the West.

On the surface it is more than a clash of cultures, more than a confrontation of races: it is a straight fight between two approaches to the world, two opposed philosophies. And under the great complexity of the structures involved – the layers of history, the mosaic of cultures – we can simplify in order to discover the major positions: one is based in secular materialism, the other in faith; one which has rejected belief altogether, the other which has placed it at the centre of its worldview. It is, therefore, not simply between Islam and the West, although many Muslims and non-Muslims who are brought up to believe in this simplistic formula will be surprised at this conclusion.

On the threshold of the 21st century the confrontation between Islam and the West poses terrible internal dilemmas for both. The test for Muslims is how to preserve the essence of the Qu'rānic message, of *adl* and *ahsan*, *ilm* and *sabr*, without it being reduced to an ancient and empty chant in our times; how to participate in the global civilization without their identity being obliterated. It is an apocalyptic test, the most severe examination. Muslims stand at the cross-roads: on the one hand they can harness their vitality and commitment in order to fulfil their destiny on the world stage, on the other hand they can dissipate their energy through internecine strife and petty bickering; harmony and hope versus disunity and disorder.

The challenge for those in the West is how to expand the Western idealistic notions of justice, equality, freedom and liberty beyond their borders to include all humanity and without appearing like 19th-century imperialists; to reach out to those not of their civilization in friendship and sincerity. In both cases a mutual understanding and working relationship are essential.

The logic of the argument demands that the West uses its great power – which includes the media – to assist in solving the long-festering problems that plague Muslim society: we have identified those of the Palestinians and Kashmiris as of the greatest urgency. There is the need to push unwilling rulers who subsist on Western arms and aid towards conceding democracy and a fairer distribution of wealth, of ensuring the rights and dignity of women and children, the less privileged and those in the minority. These problems are interwoven, binding Muslims and non-Muslims together. There can be no just and viable world order – let alone a new world order – if these wrongs are not redressed.

It is crucial, therefore, that the potential points of conflict are identified if continued confrontation is to be avoided. This is not only necessary but also possible. Into the predicament that post-modernism plunges us there is also promise. This conclusion may appear illogically optimistic in the light of the gloomy arguments above. But it is understandable in the context of the Islamic vision which is rooted firmly in history and belief. It has much to offer a world saturated with disintegration, cynicism and loss of faith. But this will only be possible if there is a universal tolerance among Muslims and non-Muslims alike of others, an appreciation of their uniqueness and a willingness to understand them. It will only be possible if this sentiment becomes both personal philosophy and national foreign policy, if it is placed on top of the agenda in preparation for the next millennium. Surely, this, too, is in the largesse of post-modernism.

– 6 –

REFOUNDING THE SECULAR STATE

Clifford Longley is a well-known journalist who has specialized since 1972 in the coverage and analysis of religious affairs. He was formerly Religious Affairs Editor of *The Times* and the *Daily Telegraph*, as well as Chief Leader Writer of *The Times* from 1990 to 1992. He now writes a regular column and leading articles for *The Tablet* and is also writing the official biography of the late Archbishop Derek Worlock.

CLIFFORD LONGLEY

DR GEOFFREY FISHER was the Archbishop of Canterbury who presided over the Coronation of Queen Elizabeth II in 1952. As he placed the Crown on her head, he said later, he felt the whole nation hold its breath.

Coronations have never been secular. In the Middle Ages theologians spoke of them virtually as an eighth sacrament, conferring on the recipient, like baptism, matrimony or ordination, a permanent religious character that could be extinguished only by death.

I am sure Dr Fisher was right in his intuition. But why did the nation hold its breath? It was because the character being conferred on the Queen in that sacred ceremony sealed the holy bonds between ruler and ruled, and therefore said something both mysterious and profound about the identity of the nation itself. It was not a contract between Queen and People. It was a covenant between Queen and God.

Yet it was a public covenant. The Coronation involved everyone, not just a few dignitaries in Westminster Abbey. It confirmed more than a Christian label on the national identity. It was more than a restatement of the constitutional fact that England is unusual among advanced countries in having a religion by law established. The Coronation enshrined at the heart of the constitution and therefore of the nation a particular set of beliefs and values. It is a mistake to see it, or the whole nexus of Church and State which it represented, as bestowing particular privileges on a particular Church community.

It was not the act of Church as Church at all; it was the act of Nation as Church. In so far as Church and Nation are not coterminous, one entity seen in two aspects, then the Church as a separate body becomes wanting. But that has been arguable since Catholic Emancipation and the repeal of the Test Acts; since, in fact, Anglicanism became voluntary, one more religious option for the citizen to choose from. And that, of course, is an irreversible change. Not to be an Anglican is no longer treason. All citizens, of whatever faith and none, have to be treated as equal. Those aspects of the British unwritten constitution which retain that earlier confessional or credal definition of nationhood, such as the role of Parliament in the affairs of the Church of England, now seem anachronistic – indeed, to those from other countries who have not been brought up with them, they seem incredible.

Other nations enshrine their core beliefs and values in their constitutions, but they do so by laws, expressed by words. They have written constitutions. Ask Americans or Frenchmen what it means to be American or French, and their reply will refer inevitably to the content of their written constitutions, the foundation documents of their state and society, as expressions of the common identity they share with their fellow countrymen.

Such constitutions take on an almost mystical value. They are not just about the nuts and bolts of the machinery of government. They define a people. They are venerated. They are the Ark of the Covenant of that society. To insult them, and the secular symbols which surround them, is to insult the honour of that society.

Britain does not have a written constitution. In England – and hence also in Scotland, Wales and Northern Ireland, despite their being excluded from the formalities of the English Church-State relationship – we have a Coronation instead. It is meant to serve the same purpose, though it serves it differently.

It gives a fundamentally unsecular character to the identity of the nation. This creates immense difficulties when the national community contains many minorities – Catholic, Jewish, Muslim, Hindu and so on – who do not share the core beliefs which that character expresses.

But the difficulties are not confined to those distinct minorities. Even greater problems occur when the majority of the nation itself starts to withdraw its explicit adherence to those beliefs. For a while, the values will survive while the beliefs decline. There will be many who regard that separation as desirable. People will want to believe that it is possible to be moral without being religious, not least because the alternative is too frightening to contemplate. They will even hail it as a kind of liberation.

But they would be foolish to regard it as stable. They would be particularly foolish to do so when they contemplate not just questions of personal morality, but the broader issues of civic identity. What answer does an Englishman give, when asked to express what it means to be English? In the closing years of the 20th century not many English people will refer back to the Coronation of 1952 for their answer, though that is the only answer the constitution can offer them.

It is here that the profoundest challenge to national identity from secularism is to be found. In all the events and collective recollections that marked the 50th anniversary of the end of the Second World War, no fact was more luminous than that those who fought and suffered in that desperate conflict were fighting and suffering for a world that has departed. The present nation, to them, has become a foreign country.

The national sense of self-confidence that made Britain such a fearsome and ultimately victorious combatant in war rested upon settled assumptions about the nature of the society they were defending. They were very much the sort of assumptions that were so vividly present in the mind of the nation in 1952, the nation that held its breath as Dr Fisher approached the throne and raised the Crown. They were natural and consensus assumptions, truths we held as so self-evident we prided ourselves in not needing to express them in writing.

They were essentially religious assumptions. The nation believed in God, and believed that God had a purpose for it. It was indeed a very special nation, which had acquired a vast international empire which was as much a moral empire as a commercial one, and it had pioneered systems of law and government which were (at least so the nation felt) the envy of the world. The Coronation of British kings and queens expressed not just a national constitution but a national vocation and sense of purpose. And this was a time when there was a still a vivid sense of the reality of nationhood. To understand the British constitution, as then conceived, it was necessary to think metaphysically, to see the hard realities behind symbols, the hard truths behind the ideas. This was a nation worth dying for. And many did.

We have lost the metaphysical imagination, largely as we have, as a nation, lost an explicit corporate faith in God. (If we do still believe in God, it is part of our private realm, nobody's business but our own.) Many of the assumptions of those who fought the war now look archaic and anachronistic, even presumptuous and arrogant. But we have been able to put very little in their place. Indeed, the fact that we have not been able to replace them with a new definition of sharing and belonging has become one of the fundamental causes of a widespread national malaise, a sullen refusal to have any sort of vision for ourselves as a people. As a result, we are witnessing the wholesale withdrawal of commitment to the entire national enterprise; and in its place, a retreat into the private worlds of do-it-yourself individual morality (which in reality is no morality at all).

The common good – a phrase at the very heart of the idea of Britishness, 50 years ago – is no longer deemed worthy of our efforts. The French and Americans can still be quite certain they know what it means to be unfrench or unamerican. But what does it mean to be unbritish? What is now the focus of British patriotism? It has come to mean little more than national selfishness.

Fortunately, the answer has not yet emerged in racial terms, though there is a real danger of that. There is a much greater danger of it emerging in the unpleasant stench of chauvinism, especially anti-Europeanism. But it is anti-Europeanism not in the name of some greater principle. Those who talk of the defence of national sovereignty never say what national sovereignty is for, what ideals the nation now stands for. If we can no longer define ourselves as British in a positive way, we can only try to define ourselves as not being French or German.

To say all this is not to criticise the way the Church of England has performed its duty as the embodiment of the national ideal. It is hard to imagine any organised system of religious belief which was capable of carrying the weight the constitution required it to carry. Indeed, in so far as it had that role, it was itself diminished by it. It was turned into a national ideology. While it may have overlapped with the Christian creed, it was by no means identical to it. The Church of England will be truer to its Christian self, the further it can pull away from that.

The reasons for the erosion of Christian faith in British society are partly similar to the reasons for that erosion in other Western liberal democracies, but partly peculiar to the unique nature of British ecclesiastical establishment. In the English settlement, the authority of Christian doctrine rested upon the authority of the

Church of England, whether it was the Church standing behind the Bible or the Church speaking for an ancient and sacred tradition. To weaken the authority of the Church is to weaken the power of the teaching the Church has to offer.

In turn, the authority of the Church of England rested largely upon its special place in the constitution, not least its being headed by the Head of State and its law being the laws approved by Parliament. Almost nobody now believes in that as a fundamental principle, but the shell of such belief is still in place, there being no substitute. But merely to disestablish the Church of England, for the sake of its own religious purity, would be to provoke an even greater national crisis. It would be necessary, at the same time, to embark upon a major work of constitutional reconstruction.

And because of the void that would be created, the Church of England could not be disestablished until the work had been completed. Once it was disestablished, however, it would be empowered afresh. It could adopt whatever relationship to the values of civic society that it wanted to. It could be a critical relationship, standing for the fundamental principle that the state cannot own everything and therefore cannot own men's souls. One of the fundamental objections to the present condition of the English State which I have as a Roman Catholic is that it claims more than any state should claim.

No state should have an established religion. Any Church which finds itself established, for historic reasons, has the most compelling reason to end that status, for the good of society and for its own good. But the Church of England has so far shown itself to be captive of its own establishment ideology, which only itself now believes in (and fewer and fewer of its own members believe in it, by all accounts). It has yet to embark on its last great duty as the Church of England: to cease to be *the* Church of England and become *a* Church of England. But it cannot just resign. Its solemn duty is to make the transition in such a way that serves the interests of the nation. It must leave behind itself, as it withdraws from its ideological role, some other, more appropriate, definition of the national identity.

The situation is this. The nation's core beliefs and values are still represented by the two key institutions, the royal family and the national church, neither of which, for various reasons, are capable of bearing the weight that is put upon them. Though the Queen herself still embodies a set of moral values, other members of her family have proved themselves no better than average. They are therefore not capable of acting as public symbols. Indeed, it is now widely recognised that it is unreasonable to expect more from them. But the constitutions' reliance on their symbolic moral role exaggerates the significance of whatever moral frailties they may be subject to, even to the extent of calling into question the survival of the monarchy itself. That is unfair, and grossly unhealthy for the good of the nation.

Secularism, as commonly understood, refers to the retreat of religious activity and belief from the public to the private domain, and its retreat from there too, in most instances. It is not religious disbelief that is the mark of secularism but religious disinterest. Secularism is peculiarly fatal to a nation like the British because it has in the past relied so heavily on religious ideas for its identity, harmony and balance.

Maybe that reliance had become untenable, and was in any case no longer compatible with the full cultural and legal equality of all citizens in a plural society. Such a society has to find new ways of expressing what all its members hold in common, and cannot rely on the universal acceptance of the truth of one religious faith or one denomination. The longer it tries to do so, the weaker it will become.

The construction of a public morality not based on explicit religious faith will be easier than the construction of a system of personal morality without faith. The difference between the two may even be that the former is quite possible while the latter is, in the end, extremely problematic. But the latter objective will be greatly helped if the former has been resolved. People are by and large not so much moral because of the teaching of a particular religion as because of the influence of those around them, members of their family, peer groups, and conspicuous members of the society to which they belong.

There is a relationship between those influences and their core beliefs, but it is by no means a simple equation. It is possible, therefore, to strengthen the moral content of those influences by measures which do not depend upon acceptance or rejection of a religious code (though the designing of those measures may have to have some relationship to such codes).

This is one of the functions that can be fulfilled by a written constitution, which can formally specify what are the fundamental rights and duties of each citizen both in relationship to the state and to their fellow citizens. It is self-supporting. Written constitutions stand alone, relying on nothing other than the general consent of the people expressed through law and through democratic institutions.

Continuity being important in these matters, such a written statement of the values at the heart of the British conception of a civilised society would need to be derived from what has existed before. These are the values which have to be enshrined in the constitution, values still represented (however inadequately, for want of better symbols) by the royal Coronation and by the Establishment of the Church of England. These have to be secularised, the institutions which represent them translated into terms which will henceforth be independent of a particular religious doctrine. Their meaning has to be extracted and written down.

The process may well seem arbitrary; and those who fundamentally reject all the moral tenets of Christianity would be bound to complain that what was happening was merely the replacement of a dogmatic framework by a legal one. But others may complain of the opposite. One can envisage a battle royal over whether to include the unborn in any constitutional guarantee of life; whether to extend full equality of rights to certain sexual lifestyles; and also whether to extend the basic protections of citizenship to refugees and immigrants, legal and otherwise.

But in the process of constructing such a public moral code, society will be facilitating the strengthening of private moral codes. Patriotism would become possible again, that is to say a healthy patriotism that consists of more than putting down the values and cultures of foreigners. Britain could become a proper nation again. And its citizens could renew their commitment to the State and to each other, the fundamental moral renewal which Britain so urgently needs.

Morality could emerge from the private parlour. The teaching of morality in schools, for instance, which is proving so bafflingly difficult, could cease to be a chase after a lowest denominator moral consensus, and could instead draw its standards from the agreed principles upon which that society was established. That is what schools used to do, when those principles were the principles of the Christian religion.

So the British have at present the worst of both worlds. They have a secular society that is peculiarly ill-equipped to be a secular society, one that does not have in place the wherewithal to manage itself as a secular society. Until this is remedied, Britain will increasingly be a sick society.

It is not a sickness that will cure itself. The first step is to name the sickness. It is not secularism, but an insufficiency of secularism. It has to go further, to become complete by acquiring a secular constitution and constitutional institutions that all can respect and believe in.

– 7 –
NEW RELIGIONS AND THE MILLENNIUM

Peter Clarke is author of eight books, including *Religion Defined and Explained* (Macmillan 1993), editor of thirteen others, and founding and present editor of the *Journal of Contemporary Religion* (Carfax Publications, Oxford). He is professor of the history and sociology of religion at King's College, London where he founded the Centre for New Religious Movements in 1982, and has been its director since then.

Peter Clarke

MILLENARIANISM is one of the most widespread and important themes in the belief system of the new religions, the most obvious example being the plethora of movements to which the umbrella term New Age Movement refers. Some New Agers believe, following the Three Ages of History theory developed by Joachim of Fiore (1145–1202), who was the inspiration behind so much medieval millenarianism, that the Age Of Aquarius, the Age of the Spirit, when Christianity will be replaced by a new religion as Christianity once replaced Judaism, is already underway while for others it is some three hundred years away. Notwithstanding this difference, all New Agers believe that through a profound inner change, society's institutions – health, education, politics – and other areas of life can be totally transformed to reflect the interconnectedness of all things and the understanding of the earth as a whole system and living entity, with humanity being a vital part of its life system.

While the eagerly awaited millennium can take many forms, underlying all of these is the sense of intense anticipation that life on earth is soon to undergo a profound transformation. In this and in other respects the millenarianism of the new religions conforms to the type of salvation which, as Cohn has shown, is generally the preoccupation of millenarian sects: the hope of such religious movements is for a salvation that will be enjoyed by the faithful as a collectivity; it will be accomplished on earth, it will be imminent and sudden, it will be total (the new era will be perfection itself) – and supernatural powers or agents will play an indispensable role in bringing it about.[1]

Millenarianism is even strongly present in new religions where least expected. For example, it has a high profile in such Hindu groups as the Brahmakumaris movement, Transcendental Meditation (TM), and it is present, albeit in a more diluted form, in the Hare Krishna movement. Among the foremost exponents of this theme among self-styled Judaeo-Christian movements are the Unification Church, the Worldwide Church of God and/or Armstrongism and its offshoot The Church of God International, and The Family (formerly The Children of God). The Atlanteans and the Aetherius society, two of the many contemporary esoteric movements, also look to the coming of a totally new dispensation as do many of the hundreds of Japanese new religions and African new movements, among them the Zionist churches of South Africa, the West African aladura or praying churches, and the African-Caribbean derived movements such as the Rastafarian movement. The phenomenon is also present in numerous Islamic and Islamic-derived movements including contemporary Sufi or mystical groups and the Nation of Islam.

Movements provide different scenarios of how precisely the present order will come to an end and why, and offer different interpretations of the form the ensuing millennium will take, who will be admitted to this new and perfect society and what

1   Cohn, N., *The Pursuit of the Millennium*, p. 13.

it will be like to live in this radically different world. Few movements are entirely consistent when it comes to their teaching about the millennium. The Brahmakumaris movement (composed of the Brahma Kumaris and the Brahma Kumars, the pure daughters and pure sons of Brahma respectively) predicts on the one hand, in the manner of a revolutionist sect, the total destruction of the present world order by divine intervention, and on the other, in the manner of a reformist sect, advocates its gradual transformation, presumably in the hope that such a catastrophe will be averted by human effort. This movement was founded by Mr Lekhraj, a well-known diamond merchant from Hyderabad, affectionately known as Dada Lekhraj, who began to receive visions in 1936 at the age of 60. One of these was a traumatic double vision involving Shiva as a point of incandescent light and cities being totally destroyed by guided missiles, later interpreted as a nuclear holocaust. Increasingly from this date, Dada Lekhraj, who was to take the name Prajapita Brahma, believed that the world had entered a climactic stage in its history: the last degenerate age of Kali Yuga was coming to an end and would terminate with a catastrophe. We are told that the end of the present order is inevitable for 'the atom and the hydrogen bombs were made for world destruction' and these instruments of catastrophe will proliferate 'until every population centre is in range of such incinerators'. Therefore, 'the final world war cannot be prevented – because it is through that war that the present evil world order will be obliterated instantly and mercifully'.[2]

Such complete destruction will be followed by a Golden Age on earth. Meanwhile, God will be extremely active in the world and all must strive to benefit from his presence. The Brahmakumaris, the heralds of the Golden Age, have the task of encouraging all to overcome body consciousness through a form of inner-worldly asceticism that includes abstinence from selfish pursuits, from material pursuits and from indulgence in sex, the most potent symbol of this state, and to live in soul consciousness. This latter state consists of realizing that one is a soul – all material and physical attributes of a person are of secondary importance – and in treating oneself and others accordingly. The Golden Age will only be for those who have previously so transformed themselves that they 'possess the power to live in utter harmony'. During the ensuing cycle of 2,500 years 'no quarrel will erupt on earth, no accident or illness will befall a single person [and] ... as much sorrow as there is in the world today so much happiness and more will be present there'.[3] Some members appear to believe that the catastrophe preceding the Golden Age can be averted. According to one informant, a teacher by profession,

> By the turn of the twenty-first century a Golden Age of peace, purity and love will have been established through the divine work initiated by Brahma Baba, our founder, who is the vehicle

2   Adi Dev, *The First Man*, 1984.
3   Ibid., pp. 235–6.

of Shiva (God) and the one who transforms and recreates souls in the image of God.[4]

In this anxiously awaited millennium, spiritually-generated environmental pollution will have been eradicated and the beauty of nature restored. Environmental pollution is essentially spiritual because our souls have been polluted through our having lost sight of who and what we are and what we are capable of achieving. In a biography of the movement's founder we read:

> Man's desperation arises from what is perceived as the human situation: we are mortal it is thought; we shall die; we live in an uncaring universe of chance. With such a world view it is little wonder that human beings have opted to get the most out of life through material acquisition and sensual pleasure. The fear of death is fertile soil in which the poison plant of greed may thrive. The ultimate thing we hunger for is love. But since we have taken ourselves for material beings, we have mistaken sex lust for love, thus exploiting each other and devaluing ourselves still further. In this desperate condition we have despoiled our home, our earth. Yet this whole chain of events was based on a single mistake. We are not mortal, after all. We are souls, non-material units of consciousness and our bodies are simply temporary earthenware costumes … We fell through the trap door of history with the fall from self-consciousness and now we have reached rock bottom. Two choices lie before us: either we clear up our act and become pure once more or we drown in a maelstrom of destruction.[5]

Thus, the present crisis has come about because we have come to accept that we are finite and without the power to preserve and protect our world. However, this strain of millenarianism clearly offers hope for this world: if we return to a life of purity, disaster can be averted and paradise can be rebuilt on earth. Through the practice of raja yoga, as interpreted by Brahma Baba, union with the Supreme Being can be realized and individuals can become channels of light, love and power. Meditation is the principle means of reaching God who as a spiritual being and the Supreme Soul cannot dwell in the material world but resides in the soul world. To realize union with God it is necessary to meditate several times each day and especially early each morning on the theme 'I am a soul and my body is a garment'. Meditation at this time is particularly important for it is early in the morning that the mind is pure and still.

There is also synchronized meditation and this is practised on the third Sunday of each month when all teachers and students in the movement throughout the world meditate at the same time; linked together in this way they generate a greater amount of pure, saving energy than when meditating either alone or in local groups and the revitalizing, saving energy produced is transmitted to the world in the form of vibrations. Purity is the key to self and world transformation, and while there is no vow as such either of chastity or celibacy individuals are given 'advice' about the disadvantages of sex which is presented as the most serious impediment to reach-

---

4   Ibid.
5   Ibid., p. 262–3.

ing the highest levels of spirituality and enlightenment. Guided by this advice and persuaded of its truth some members, including a number of married people, have in fact taken the vow of celibacy. It is taught that sexual love fosters possessiveness and jealousy; directing love towards one person demands a partner that lives up to expectations, one that is perfect, and when this does not happen there is anger. In contrast, spiritual love knows no possessiveness or anger and frees one to do much more, gives one more physical energy, more concentration, a better quality of thought and a better sense of well being.

According to Brahmakumaris teaching, purity is an essential prerequisite for full participation in the establishment of the millennium and for the full enjoyment of that paradise. The contrast between this approach to the millennium and that of other Eastern-derived movements such as the Rajneesh Foundation and self-styled Christian movements, among them the Unification Church and/or the Moonies and The Children of God and/or The Family of Love could not be more striking.

If the Brahmakumaris movement bears a certain resemblance to the *Catharist Perfecti* who dominated the religious life of a large part of southern France and northern Italy for more than fifty years, The Family of Love, in its early days bore a close resemblance, especially in the area of moral antinomianism, to the medieval Free Spirit or Spiritual Liberty movement, a movement that exercised even greater influence on medieval western Europe than the Catharist sect. The Family of Love was founded in California in 1967 by David Berg, alias Moses David. He initially preached that beginning in 1968 the world would be engulfed by a series of natural and man-made disasters leading to the advent of the anti-Christ. Only those prepared to condemn and abandon the whole system of Western values, to become 'anti-systemites', would survive the impending apocalypse to rule over the future earthly paradise which would follow in its wake. One of the MO letters (official despatches sent by the leader to the members of the movement) predicts that 'The white powers of the Western world are about to collapse under the rising red tide of color … the white man's Doomesday impends'. This was in 1971 and during the next decade a Communist regime under the authority of the anti-Christ was to arise and with it would come the persecution of the few remaining faithful Christians during the period of the Great Tribulation. Christ was expected to destroy the anti-Christ in 1993 and thereby mark the beginning of the millennium which would finally culminate in the destruction of Satan and the judgement of all mankind. The righteous were then to inhabit a heavenly city for all eternity. This brand of millenarianism was characterized not only by an attack on Western values and institutions but also by its strong anti-Semitic feeling which increased in intensity after Berg's unsuccessful visit to Israel in 1970.[6]

---

6   David, Moses, *Mo Letters*, p. 681.

Berg presented himself as the mouthpiece of God with a mission to save the faithful from impending destruction and he saw fit to pursue this goal with every means both fair and foul – those who refused to listen to him were deemed to have forfeited all saving grace. As God's chosen instrument Berg could do no wrong nor could he be prevented from fulfilling his mission by mere man-made laws, norms and taboos. These restrictive and inhibiting devices were only for sinners whereas for the just, such as himself, all things were lawful, a contemporary version of the previously mentioned medieval doctrine of the Free Spirit. As the mouthpiece of God, Berg was the recipient of the divinely revealed 'Law of Love' which, unlike the Mosaic law which condemned fornication and adultery, made it a matter of faith to reflect and embody God's love in all things, fornication and adultery included. Part of this revealed 'Law of Love' was the strategy of 'Flirty Fishing' which consisted essentially in members attracting converts to the movement through sexual intercourse.[7] With the benefit of hindsight some ex-members are astonished not only that they participated in this way of life but that they actually believed it to be true and divinely sanctioned. Deborah Davis, Moses David's daughter, has written of how her father as founder and leader of Familiy – still known as the Children of God Family at the time she wrote – was 'given over to evil' and she explains her own participation and that of others in such evil thus:

> To doubt Mo's (David Berg's) revelations would be to doubt the miraculous circumstances that had brought each disciple to learn at the feet of God's Prophet. Each one of us believed we had been led there by the very hand of God. How wonderful, how marvellous![8]

After leaving she was unable to believe that it had all happened to her but for the fact that, 'Every day I am surrounded by the living scars and wounds which assure me that it is all true'.[9] What made it easy for her, she explains, was the belief that she was the daughter of the 'End Time Prophet'; in other words, her belief in the imminence of the millennium which had 'great spiritual dividends and gave great support to one's self image'. However, what finally brought about her total disillusion with the movement and was to prove intolerable was the realization over time that the 'Law of Love' was in fact a law of 'rebellion, of hatred, of no mercy and no forgiveness'.[10]

While completely different in their views on sexuality and in their rules governing sexual behaviour, the sexual asceticism of the Brahmakumaris and the sexual licence of the Children of God are symbolically two sides of the same coin. In the case of the former, extreme sexual asceticism can not only act as a powerful instru-

---

7 Wallis, R., *The Elementary Forms*, p. 17.
8 Davis, Deborah, *The Children of God*, p. 188.
9 Ibid., p. 66.
10 Ibid., p. 67.

ment of social cohesion and control but also constitute a complete rejection of prevailing moral norms pointing to the advent of a totally transformed world founded on a new morality. In the case of the latter, the radical smashing of sexual and other taboos by Moses David on the scale reported by his daughter, as in similar antinomian sects, was likewise a powerful means of control and social integration. While it is most frequently interpreted as a sordid venture in unbridled eroticism, it is also symbolic of an onslaught on the past and of an urge to give birth to a completely new way of living.

The Worldwide Church of God and/or Armstrongism, founded by the late Herbert W. Armstrong, at one time an advertising salesman, has been using its own television and radio network, press and publications for over forty years to put across its own particular prophetic message about the imminent end of the world and the advent of God's kingdom. In 1956 a key booklet *1975 in Prophecy*, replete with spine-chilling illustrations of the Great Tribulation, was offered to the public. One illustration carries the caption, ' … and during the Great Tribulation with its fiendish tortures people will die so rapidly there will be need of mass graves. Here you see thousands of bodies being buried in a ravine.' Citing prophecy after prophecy from the Old and New Testaments, *1975 in Prophecy* predicts the return of the Nazis to power, a devastating drought between 1965-72, and the 'Ten Nation European Colossus' striking the cities of the United States and the United Kingdom (the descendants of the latter being the descendants of the Ancient Israelites) with hydrogen bombs and reducing the inhabitants to slavery. Another 1956 brochure bore the title *United States heading for Total Collapse in Twenty Short Years*. The Great Tribulation and attendent disasters were to come about because 'Christianity' in the form of the established historic Christian churches, while they had appropriated the name of Christ, had distorted his message, in particular his teaching about the advent of the Kingdom and its physical, this-worldly location and had rebelled against his laws.

By 1975, as we have seen, The Great Tribulation was to have happened and the millennium to have been in place but as that year drew nearer, the content of the booklet *1975 in Prophecy* became problematic. Armstrong, meanwhile, reportedly defended himself by stating that although some people interpreted him in that way he neither set a definite date for the End and the onset of the millennium nor predicted that they would definitely happen but simply cautioned that they were a possibility. Undeterred by the uneventful arrival and passing of 1975 the church carried on proclaiming on its television and radio stations in the United States, Australia, the Caribbean, South America and Europe, and through its magazine *The Plain Truth* that the millennium was nigh and would be established after the Great Tribulation. This movement, like so many others, is emphatic that the faithful will be granted their final reward not in some other-worldly paradise but on this earth. It states:

> There is not a shred of evidence that Jesus or the Apostles envisaged 'heaven' as the final state of the saved. Had not Jesus promised the meek that they would inherit the earth? (*Matt.* 5: 5). If he (Jesus) had wished to teach heaven as the reward of the faithful, this would have required a specific contradiction of the Old Testament which had envisaged a new earth as the scene of the messianic salvation. The message is no different when we come to the reign of Christ and his saints as described in the sublime prophecy of Revelation 20. For here too the scene is still the earth, where the nations 'in the four corners of the earth go up on the breath of the earth and encompass the camp of the saints and fire comes down from heaven. (*Rev.* 20: 9).[11]

It insists that however much the established churches might distort this teaching by spiritualizing the future reign of God the 'plain truth' is that Jesus's thousand year reign of peace will take place here on earth.[12] The Worldwide Church of God, like Christian fundamentalism, is very clearly in opposition to the tendency prevalent among theologians and biblical scholars to interpret much of the scriptures symbolically. This movement's emphasis on the literal, concrete meaning of scripture and its aggressive and hostile attack on the 'spiritualizing' of this by theologians is a constant refrain in all its teaching and writings. On the question of reward and punishment, for example, it points out that individuals and nations who fail to adhere to the teaching of Jesus will be punished by physical adversity and that this will be the only path to God and happiness left open to them.

In Unificationist or Moonie thinking also, now is the time for the establishment of the millennium on earth. The mission of the Second Messiah is, under the guidance of the Holy Spirit, to restore to people the complete understanding of their full nature and of their relationship to God. The Holy Spirit or the Spirit of Truth can, it is believed, speak more effectively through Moon than through anyone else. The sacred text of the Moonies, the *Divine Principle*, consists of communications which Moon received from God the Father, the Holy Spirit, Jesus and other spiritual beings. Though God the Father, the Holy Spirit and Jesus constitute the Trinity, only God the Father is God and/or divine. Like so many other new religions the Unification Church sees itself as 'perfecting' the teachings of the great religious traditions, particularly Christianity. Eventually all Christians will be united around his teachings and even all religions, a goal pursued by new religions of non-Christian origin including the Sathya Sai Baba movement of Indian origin, the Japanese new religion Agonshu (Japanese for the Sanskrit term *agama*) and Kofuku no Kagaku (The Science of Human Happiness) of Japan.

The millenarianism of the Moonies can only be understood in the context of the movement's teachings about the Fall which differ fundamentally from that of Chris-

---

11 Buzzard, A.F., *Kingdom of God – Where and When?*, pp. 12–13.
12 Ibid.

tianity. According to the *Divine Principle*, in creating Adam and Eve God intended that in due course they should marry and become the True Parents whose offspring would begin the process of populating the earth. The Trinity of God, Adam the True Father and Eve the True Mother would be realized. The Three Blessings would be bestowed on Adam and Eve and their descendants if the proper relationships were developed between husband and wife, parents and children, creatures and the cosmos and between all of these and God. The first of these blessings was to consist of the ability to achieve perfection, the second, the creation of an Ideal Family and the third, human mastery over the whole of creation. But this plan failed to fully materialize on account of Archangel Lucifer's misuse of the greatest of all powers, that of love; jealous of God's love for Adam he began an illicit emotional and sexual relationship with Eve which produced a totally corrupt trinity of false parents consisting of Satan and Adam and Eve, which brought about the Fall.

From that time onwards history has consisted of a succession of attempts by God and his chosen human agents, including Jesus, to reverse the effects of the Lucifer-centred relationship which resulted from this forbidden union and which gave rise to original sin inherited by all, and to establish on earth the original Kingdom of Heaven, a Kingdom of complete harmony and perfection. Had Jesus married he would have accomplished this but he was crucified before he could do so. What he did manage to provide was the means to full spiritual salvation. But the need remained for complete salvation which has an equally important physical dimension and it is the task of another Messiah, the Lord of the Second Coming, also referred to as both the Second Messiah and the Third Adam, to accomplish this. The Second Messiah has come. He was allegedly born in Korea sometime between 1917 and 1930, and many in the Unification Church believe him to be their leader, the Reverend Sun Myung Moon. This Messiah has received the first blessing, is free of original sin, as are his children, and he has the power to remove this sin from the souls of the children whose parents he blesses in marriage. The advent of the Kingdom is not inevitable, it would appear. Preconditions include the triumph of the ideology of love over all others, particularly Communism, through strenuous and committed evangelization, but should they prove necessary, weapons must be used to accomplish this.

Moreover, Moonies believe, like Scientology and the Self Religions generally, that human beings were created with the potential for perfection in order to enjoy the pleasures of nature, fulfil themselves and glorify God. This threefold purpose was, as previously noted, frustrated by the Fall and will only now be possible when the right conditions have been re-established for the original father-child relationship. This restoration entails an awareness of God's plans such as procreation in a God-centred marriage so that the experience of mutual love in such a family can reactivate the true God-man relationship on an ever-widening scale. In time harmonious relationships will be formed throughout the whole of God's creation thereby fulfilling its purpose. The formation of restored families is an absolutely fundamental tenet of Unification Church theology of the millennium, for without this all else would fail. Moreover, it is this premise that lies behind the mass marriage ceremony which is the only sacrament and the one essential religious belief and practice of the movement and most important condition for the transformation of the human race and its projection onto a higher plane of spirituality. In this way the Lord of the Second Coming must complete the establishment of the original unrealized Trinity, consisting of God, the True Father Adam and the True Mother Eve.

The Unification Church in believing that the Lord of the Second Coming has already arrived is in this sense a pre-millennialist movement while those who believe that the second advent will follow the millennium are essentially post-millennialists. Pre-millennialists are not unanimous on how the millennium will come about but most tend to accept that it will be realized by divine cataclysmic action, while the post-millennialist, likewise not all of one mind on this, are generally of the view that the millennium will come about more gradually through a combination of human agency and divine intervention. Some movements, among them Transcendental Meditation (TM), include elements from both tendencies. In 1972, TM's founder, Maharishi Mahesh Yogi, inaugurated his 'World Plan' in order 'to solve the age old problems of mankind in this generation [through] bringing enlightenment to the peoples of every country'. This was to be achieved through the application of the 'Science of Creative Intelligence' (CI): when individuals use their CI then a 'fulfilled society' will arise in which the human race will be free from suffering. CI, for its part, could be developed by the regular practice of TM which consists of 'a simple effortless mental technique' and would enable individuals 'to act spontaneously in the light of all knowledge' and thus enrich all aspects of life. While the Worldwide Church of God was predicting that 1975 was to be the year of annihilation of the present order, TM proclaimed the same year to be the 'Dawn of the Age of Enlightenment' and assured all that a 'global transformation' was already under way, that the negativity which had been dominating the world had begun to decline and that the value of life according to natural law, the new master key to replace CI, was now emerging in every country simultaneously – in other words, the ideal society was in the process of being born.

The timing of the advent of the millennium or new and totally transformed society was explained at this stage, 1975, in terms of 'the eternal cycle of natural law'. In this cycle the extent to which the natural law is lived out in daily life declines over time from its maximum or 100% level to its minimum level of zero at which point its full potential is reawakened. In one generation the natural law can leap forward from zero to 100% and, according to TM, the generation fortunate enough to experience this upward surge is the present one. This great leap forward takes us into the millennial age where 'As long as 100% value of natural law is lived in daily life ... society is ideal and nations invincible. The family of nations enjoys perfect health in every way. The administration of society is so perfect and automatic that it is unseen ...'.[13] And it was claimed that in 1978 world peace had been partially achieved by sending *siddhas* (teachers) to practise TM in troubled areas.

TM adds a new dimension to expressions of millenarianism in teaching that there is nothing inherently permanent about this millennial state nor is it as yet universal. If it is to persist and to embrace all people, the TM formula must be applied; according to this a minimum of 10,000 people must practise meditation and 100 in every million respectively. In the absence of a sufficient number to ensure the persistence of an ideal world the World Government instituted a pilot project to create 'models of an ideal society' in twenty of the larger countries and eighty-eight of the smaller ones. They measured the progress made towards the ideal society according to the amount of positive news reported in the press as charted by the 'Ideal Society Index'. TM claimed that all the signs were that the ideal society was being established on a much wider scale as a result of the practice of its technique of meditation.

Aum Shinri-kyo is the name most observers will associate with contemporary Japanese millenarianism but virtually every Japanese new religion – and there are several hundred – without exception either is or has been emphatically millenarian, albeit in different ways. For Tenrikyo (Religion of Heavenly Truth) founded by Niki Nakayama (1798–1886) who claimed to be the 'shrine of God' and the mediatrix between God and the human race, the heavenly kingdom, located in this world, was to be one in which there was to be complete peace and happiness and a total absence of pain and suffering. Sokka Gakkai (Value Creation Society), the largest and politically most powerful of the Japanese new religions, both in Japan and abroad, envisages the establishment of a Buddhahood as a concrete reality and this conviction is very often expressed in terms of a New Age of world peace. As one member stated,

> Through a fundamental change or inner reformation that comes from chanting, the causes for war and violence, which exist within all human beings, can be transformed into positive tendencies towards peace and harmony and this human revolution in as many human beings as possible is the only way of securing lasting peace. Furthermore this enlightened state within the life of the individual will reflect out onto the environment and save it. *This lasting peace and harmony will be achieved in this world*.[14] (author's italics)

However, Soka Gakkai's optimism is tempered with a strong element of the apocalyptic. It laments the destruction of the environment and attributes this to the widely-

---

13 Posner, 'Transcendental Meditation, Perfect Health and the Millennium' in *Sickness and Sectarianism*, p. 100.

14 Causten, R., *Nichirin Shoshyu Buddhism*, pp. 293–4.

entertained but wrong-headed notion people have of the individual self. The movement's President, Daisaku Ikeda, has depicted contemporary society as an 'ocean of flames' and went on to provide a moral explanation for this:

> It is a pity to see how our modern civilization has been dominated by man's individual self and has been developed without any control. Man's greed has disturbed the environment, tapped much of the oil resources and constructed a gigantic technological civilization. Large skyscrapers, swift means of communication, unnatural food and terrible atomic weapons are signs that man is attached to earthly and materialistic greed. There is no doubt that mankind will be destroyed if man is dehumanized in this way.[15]

The solution lies in the version of Buddhism taught by the 13th-century Buddhist monk, Nichiren Daishonin (1222–1282), which is the inspiration behind Soka Gakkai. Nichiren's teachings are themselves replete with apocalyptic gloom; he was convinced that his mission was that of the Boddhisattva Jogyo who in the Lotus Sutra was commissioned with propagating the True Law in the Latter Day. Later he was to relinquish this role and declare himself to be the original Buddha and the Buddha of the Latter Day of the law. Sekaikyuseikyo, The Church of World Messianity, predicts that heaven is about to be realized on earth and has accordingly and appropriately named its journal *Heaven on Earth*. Moreover, it has established a model of the paradise it expects to see established, a practice followed by many Japanese new religions. But before the advent of the millennium there is to be a period of crisis through which only the pure will pass unscathed, that is those who conform their behaviour to the divine laws or 'The Way'. This conformity is centred on the correct comportment in social relationships, including relationships with the dead and with Nature. Once again the precarious state of the world is explained largely in terms of human greed and mistreatment of the environment resulting from false notions of the self. An unpolluted environment, peace and sound health of mind and body can only be had through a new beginning in a new order brought about through a radical change in our understanding of the nature of the self and of its potential. Traditional religious systems are regarded as in large measure responsible for the catastrophe in which the world now finds itself.

When we look for satisfactory general interpretations of millenarianism it is still very much a question of seeing 'through a glass darkly'. There are no convincing explanations of a general kind that will enable us to understand what gives rise to such a potent mixture of deep foreboding and unbridled optimism. Social or social-psychological interpretations broadly relate it to three factors: a period of crisis and upheaval, feelings of anxiety and insecurity and a deprived or oppressed class. Elements of the first two are found in many millenarian movements with crisis and upheaval often giving rise to anxiety and insecurity. If deprivation is taken to mean material deprivation this would seem to be less useful as a tool of explana-

---

15 Ikeda, D., *A Lasting Peace*, p. 99.

tion. At best it fits only certain cases. Evidence from Japan and elsewhere suggests that where the new religions are concerned, stress and strain theories and those that have recourse to notions of profound social dislocation and cultural confusion fare somewhat better. Explanations for the rise of the millenarian movement, Aum Shinrikyo, accused of the sarin gas attack on the Tokyo underground in 1995, include the interpretation that its apocalyptic obsession is in part a response to the failure of Japan to ensure that its spiritual civilization kept up with its material civilization.

But it should not be forgotten that happiness and joy are just as capable of producing a longing for the millennium as are anxiety, stress and spiritual poverty. Whatever the psychological state of the millenarian, and the social conditions, historical, geographical and religious settings in which they may find themselves, two aspects of the millenarian belief are, it would seem, fairly constant and universal: first of all it is a powerful means of recruitment in the hands of a charismatic prophet or founder of a religion and, secondly, it both legitimizes and provides an effective ideology of total and complete change for those, whatever their predispositions and goals, who believe that the present state of society is intolerable. More positively, like mountaineers and others who pit themselves against the limits that the natural environment imposes, millenarians struggle against the widespread tendency found, even among believers, to settle down in the present and accept that the frustrations of the human condition cannot be removed. It has at times been millenarians not realists who have explored the complexities of human life and the range of human possibilities and have provided visions of a better order of existence which, although often bizarre in the extreme and sometimes destructive at the individual and group level, make the important point: that none of us can live without some image of what a better world would be.

Bibliography

E. ALLEN, 'Religious Heterodoxy and Nationalist Tradition: The Continuing Evolution of the Nation of Islam' in *New Trends and Developments in the World of Islam*, Peter Clarke (ed.) (London, Luzac Oriental, 1997)

E. BARKER, *The Making of a Moonie* (Oxford, Basil Blackwell, 1984)

A.F. BUZZARD, *The Kingdom of God – Where and When?* (Texas, Church of God International)

R. CAUSTEN, *Nichirin Shoshu Buddhism*, (London, Rider, 1988)

PETER CLARKE and J. SOMERS, *Japanese New Religions in the West*, (Eastbourne, Kent, Curzon Press/Japan Library, 1994)

N. COHN, *The Pursuit of the Millennium* (London, Paladin, 1970)

MOSES DAVID, *Mo Letters*, 1978

D. DAVIS, *The Children of God, Grand Rapids*, (Michigan, Zondervan Books, 1984)

ADI DEV, *The First Man*, (Mount Abu, Prajapita Brahma – Kumaris Uiversity, 1983)

R. ELLWOOD, *TenriKyo. A Pilgrimage Faith, Tenri*, (Nara, Tenri University, 1982)

P. HEELAS, 'Self Religions' in *The Study of Religion, Traditional and New Religions* (eds) Stewart Sutherland and Peter Clarke (London, Routledge, 1991) pp. 167-174

D. IKEDA, *A Lasting Peace*, (New York and Tokyo, Weatherhill, 1981)

T. POSNER, 'Transcendental Meditation, Perfect Health and the Millennium' in *Sickness and Sectarianism* (ed.) K. Jones, (Aldershot, Hants, Gower, 1985), pp. 94-113

R. WALLIS, *The Elementary Forms of the New Religious Life*, (London: Routledge, 1984)

– 8 –

LIVING WITH THE QUESTIONS

Psychotherapy and the Myth of Self-Fulfilment

Howard Cooper is an analytic psychotherapist in private practice, a rabbi, and a lecturer in Biblical, psychological and spiritual themes. A graduate of the Leo Baeck College, he is the editor of *Soul Searching: Studies in Judaism and Psychotherapy* (SCM Press, 1988) and is co-author of *A Sense of Belonging: Dilemmas of British Jewish Identity* (Weidenfeld & Nicholson, 1991).

HOWARD COOPER

TWO CHEERS FOR SECULARISM

I

> Literature is where I go to explore the highest and lowest places in human society and in the human spirit, where I hope to find not absolute truth but the truth of the tale, of the imagination and of the heart.
>
> Salman Rushdie,
> 1989

THE PSYCHOTHERAPIST'S ART, like that of the novelist, is a fictive endeavour. It is a way of telling stories that makes some people feel better, some of the time. This may be because, when it works, it evokes – or creates – 'the truth ... of the imagination and of the heart'; and in doing so manages to navigate between the Scylla and Charybdis of our interior lives: the wish for the seductive, comforting security of 'absolute truth' and the fear of being overwhelmed by a spiralling descent into meaninglessness.

Yet the psychotherapist's methods, like those of the novelist, are rigorously disciplined. A deep and exacting training, embracing theoretical concepts and self-understanding, is combined with a diligent attentiveness to what goes on in oneself, in the other, between oneself and the other, moment by moment. Such craftsmanship is what enables therapy to approach 'the truth ... of the heart', which is a mystery.

But this truth-telling, truth-revealing enterprise should not be sentimentalized. The therapist shares with the historian a working hypothesis: that it is by analysing and interpreting past experience – and for the therapist, the immediate experience – that individuals, like societies, are enabled to understand the contradictions of their past and to come to terms with the complexities of their present.

Nevertheless, immersed as we are in subjectivity and the pluralistic nature of interpretation, there remains – or should remain – a degree of provisionality about the whole thing. The Japanese film-maker Kurosawa, in his early masterpiece *Roshomon* – where the same event is filmed from the four different perspectives of the protagonists – gave cinematic expression to this key article of modernist faith: the recognition that human knowledge is subjective and indeterminate. The artist accepts that, as Rushdie puts it, 'all that is solid *has* melted into air, that reality and morality are not givens but imperfect human constructs'. This is 'the point from which fiction begins'. And psychotherapy too, in its attempts to create healing fictions for those who choose to, or are driven to, 'explore the highest and lowest places' within themselves.

Modern psychoanalytically-informed therapy makes no claim to unearth *the* truth about past events in a person's history. What it can do is help to construct a narrative, or series of narratives, about what might have happened, and what the consequences of what might have happened might have been. This is – in spite of Freud's insistence that he was discovering objective truths about the human mind – more like an art than a science. As that great novelist in the sky recognized when presenting us in the opening chapters of Genesis with two complementary accounts of the creation of the world, there is more than one way to tell a story.

Although science and scientific investigation became for Freud (as the analyst Adam Phillips has expressed it) 'the method he believes to be most exempt from wishfulness, and therefore the most truthful', the therapist who listens to the story which unfolds in the consulting room is aware, as with any narrative, that there are gaps in the information provided, repetitions which are not repetitious, ambiguities, contradictions and paradoxes. What creates tension in a story is partly the way that words are linked together to make the visible action of the story; but it is also the things that are left out, that are implied, the landscape just under the smooth (but sometimes broken and unsettled) surface of things.

Together, the therapist and the patient learn to read, decipher interpret the multidimensional texts of a person's life – and this includes listening in to the silences and the gaps between the words – and to do so with as much attention and sensitivity as both can muster. Such thinking together can help create a set of stories about our own lives. And the themes of these stories which we construct – and reconstruct – can help us develop a framework for understanding why we may experience life in the ways that we do.

But this fictive enterprise is not an exercise in problem-solving. If it has curative properties, if it helps alleviate human distress and dis-ease, this may be because such psychoanalytically-informed story-telling involves a particular kind of intimacy. It is the intimacy of a conversation in which everything is permitted to enter into thought, and nothing need be censored – and where the temptation to censor is itself of interest within the conversation. It is the potentially reparative intimacy of a relationship between two people – separate but together – striving to create a shared language of feeling.

Such psychotherapy is sustainable as a craft only through acts of faith: faith in oneself, faith in the process – that a patient and attentive waiting will enable 'the pattern to emerge' (Freud) and faith that the uniquely secret, unknown and unknowable parts of the other are yet part of a shared humanity which can be reached through interpretative dialogue.

This 'secular' faith is, however, resistant to certainties. It is wary of reductive 'answers' or totalizing 'explanations'. It tries to avoid the hubris attendant on presuming to know 'the truth'. Therapists tend to be wary of omnipotent stances – human or divine. An interpretation which illuminates an emerging pattern of a person's life may throw other patterns into darkness. Omnipotent quests for self-knowledge fail to respect the ever-renewed elusiveness of the unconscious, subverter of intelligibility. We are so much more than our means to know give us to know.

So, paradoxically, the secular craft of psychotherapy requires its practitioners to develop an attitude of humility in the face of the mystery of who we are, a reverence for the individual perhaps more often associated with 'religion' than 'secularism'. Yet at the same time, to pursue the Delphic injunction 'Know thyself' may involve calling into question a cherished belief in the inherent goodness and unlimited perfectibility of the individual. Our ingrained narcissism, rooted in the early infant-experience of self-centredness, can express itself creatively in relationships and in worldly achievements, but it also has destructive potential. Indeed the denial of our innate destructiveness leads to psychologies which transform the self-denying admonition 'Know thyself' into the pseudo-liberating appeal of 'To thine own self be true'.

Under the guise of promoting 'self-expression' and offering the seductive, painless possibility of discovering one's 'human potential' or 'true self' in the 'here and now', some of the newer, less intellectually rigorous brands of post-analytic therapy can covertly promote a selfish and carefree, (i.e. careless), 'me-first' individualism. At their root lies the fantasy that life could be unconditioned, self-gratifying and permissive of our unrestrained desires. This omnipotent denial of personal limitations involves a wish to avoid the distressing sense of powerlessness evoked by the normal, inevitable disappointments of life. In the attempt to circumvent such frustrations, therapeutic fundamentalism offers salvation now. But to confront the abyss within ourselves and control its chaos is a time-consuming and often painful task. The discipline required is akin to that traditionally associated with religion at its best: a lifelong caring attention to the small details of daily life.

'Self-realization', 'self-actualization', total 'self-fulfilment' – and all the so-called 'therapies' and 'self-help' guides and books which promote these specious goals – have replaced the worn-out certainties of conventional religious faith with the similarly illusory certainties of a secular theology. Such 'feel good' approaches to 'personal growth' tend to fight shy of Freud's darker, ironic understanding that he was taking away neuroses so that people could get on with the ordinary unhappiness of daily life. Such pessimism, it seems, can be too much to bear.

> Go, go, go, said the bird: human kind
> Cannot bear very much reality.
>
> T.S. Eliot,
Four Quartets

II

> If there are Jews who have begun to find the stories the novelists tell more provocative and pertinent than the sermons of some of the rabbis, perhaps it is because there are regions of feeling and consciousness in them which cannot be reached by the oratory of self-congratulation and self-pity.
>
> Philip Roth,
> *Writing About Jews*, 1963

THERAPISTS, like novelists, find themselves mapping out previously unexplored 'regions of feeling and consciousness'. They reach the parts others, including moralizing religious leaders, cannot reach. For they take seriously, yet without inducing guilt, the fact that within the human psyche a Promethean battle wages between our experiences of love and hate, hope and despair, contentment and desperation, fullness and emptiness, comfort and distress, nurture and abandonment. These basic polarities of our instinctual life form our psychological make-up from the earliest moments of our existence. The conflicts between these opposing states-of-mind-and-being become part of the fabric of our experience of being alive in the world, the warp and weft of everyday life. But how are we to make sense of what we experience, pulled as we are from birth onwards between creative and destructive impulses?

Psychoanalysis, like religion, is a vast meaning-generating system. Whether the meaning lies in God's hands or within the unconscious, both systems are huge intellectual enterprises designed to cajole us into viewing life as being composed of events which have meaning. Both suggest that everything that we do and everything that happens to us is part of a larger picture, of which we can only know a part. Both help us defend ourselves against the terrifying alternative: meaninglessness.

Like the psychoanalytic myth, the mythologies and theologies of the monotheistic faiths are immensely creative attempts to deal with the potentially overwhelming, annihilatory anxiety of *tohu va'vohu* : the formless, chaotic black hole at the very beginning of Genesis – which is analogous to (and a metaphor for) aspects of early infantile experience. Within the myth, God fills the emptiness with creative activity, just as we have to fill our lives with acts of creativity (and love?) to generate meaning in the face of the void.

From infancy onwards we form defences to keep out the potentially overwhelming forces of chaos within us, sea-walls to resist the battering of the raging seas. As we develop, and through the process of socialization and education, we find ways of containing or transforming these elemental energies within ourselves. But this work is bruising and exhausting. And for many it is confusing beyond belief. Western religions attempt to create a safe haven, a framework of thought and action within which the believer can find sustenance, guidance and security, while the battle between our creative and destructive capacities, between 'good' and 'evil', is being waged.

Thus the obvious attraction of religious systems, institutions and leaders offering clear answers to the confusions and passions of life. The capacity to tolerate uncertainty and ambivalence – the hallmark of mature psychological health – is in distinct tension with religious standpoints which offer unqualified definitions of what is true and what is false, of what is good practice and what is bad faith.

Psychotherapy, however, starts with no *a priori* moral belief that an individual is born either in original sin or with an innate goodness. In this sense at least, it is an avowedly secular discipline. But it is a moral activity to the extent that it recognizes that human beings are, from their earliest moments onwards, dependent, symbol-forming, myth-making creatures, seeking security, containment and human contact in the face of potentially devastating inner experiences of neediness, helplessness and despair. Traditionally, religion has attempted to address these needs and feelings, yet has invariably done so without understanding their origins within an individual's early psychological development, nor the unconscious power such feelings exert within adult life.

The psychotherapist knows that in our formative years we feel, and are, vulnerable and defenceless. As babies, toddlers, young children, we each go through experiences – unique to ourselves but sharing certain characteristics with everyone else – in which we feel varying degrees of emotional distress caused by anything from hunger, to the pain of abandonment, rejection or humiliation, to verbal violence, or physical abuse. Whether the experiences are at the hands of a parent, other family members, schoolmates, or strangers, we have all experienced moments, hours, days, when we were frightened, neglected, taunted or abused; the victim of someone we experienced as having more power than us, or control over us, an authority too strong to defeat. This plethora of experiences constitute a distinct pain-filled subtext to our own personal history.

These experiences and memories are still inside us, alive and potent, whether we are consciously aware of them or not. We have also survived these experiences, more or less. This is partly because we had other experiences which softened the harshness, which soothed the terrors and distress; and partly because our developing psyche – with its instinctive striving for the preservation of life – found ways of sealing off these experiences from consciousness, and thereby defending ourselves from the emotional pain of what was happening to us, and in us.

It is our capacity to survive what we experience without psychologically disintegrating, or falling into total despair, which makes us into human beings who can also hope, dream, and imagine a future which is different from the past. Our capacity to project hope into the future is a primary means of surviving experiences of powerlessness and helplessness. The process of projection is as fundamental for survival on the psychological level, as is breathing on the biological level. Through projection we create meaning; but projective processes can be benign or malign.

To project hope into the future includes being able to imagine that we now have the capacity to make things happen the way we want them to. Gradually, we feel that we can move from being the victim of distressing circumstances to being the author of our own lives, exercising a degree of control over what happens to us. But this transformation contains a psychological danger. As Freud's great partner and eventual rival, the psychologist C.G. Jung, realized: 'It is the persecuted ones who persecute'.

For as we move towards a sense of autonomy we still carry within us all the feelings that went with our experience of victimhood. And that means we contain a rage, a wish to punish, a wish for revenge, a murderous wish to destroy, a wish to inflict on others the pain we have experienced – which we may not even be conscious of having experienced. And if we remain unconscious of these impulses we will be compelled to act them out. We become the persecutors.

There are many impulses within ourselves which may feel unacceptable, or which we have been told are unacceptable, which then become feelings liable to be projected onto others so that we do not have to experience them ourselves. As well as murderous and destructive fantasies, there are feelings like greed, lust, envy, possessiveness, the wish to control others, the wish for attention, the wish to get our own way: many complex emotional states which it can be difficult to accept are part of ourselves or to contain within ourselves. Failure to recognize these feelings leads to them being acted out in aggressive or violent fashion, or projected outside of ourselves onto others, whom we will then feel are threatening us with these very same things.

Many of these feelings swirl around 'ordinary' family life, as Philip Larkin's refrain testifies:

> They fuck you up, your mum and dad
> They may not mean to, but they do.
> They fill you with the faults they had
> And add some extra, just for you.[1]

As psychotherapists discover every day in a secular, psychological sense, 'the sins of the fathers are visited on the children to the third or fourth generation'; the emotional hurt of one generation is transmitted to the next generation, who in turn unconsciously re-enact unresolved emotional conflicts in relation to their own children. This cycle of deprivation is rooted in the inability to contain or transform 'unacceptable' feelings.

Sometimes these feelings are projected in malign fashion onto groups: 'greedy' Jews, 'fanatical' Muslims, 'self-righteous' Christians, 'dirty' Gypsies, 'immoral' homosexuals, 'scrounging' beggars, immigrants and single mothers, 'evil' children …

---

1 Larkin, Philip, *High Windows*, 'This Be The Verse'. Quoted by permission: Faber & Faber Ltd

Our capacity to demonize is endless and endlessly destructive.

Religious traditions have proved particularly susceptible to such emotionally-regressed thinking, in particular the continual pull towards splitting the world into self-contained opposites – good and bad, us and them, secular and religious, heaven and hell, believers and heretics, my way or else. The internal unconscious processes of splitting and projection provide a much sought-after sense of security. We know where we are. We know what is what. The simplicity of 'either/or' usually feels safer than the ambivalence of 'both/and'.

Religion is not alone of course in offering such consolation. Collective modes of thinking dominated by these unconscious forces are omnipresent: xenophobia within nation-states also involves the malign projection of parts of the self which we wish to disavow. Whether in personal relationships, family life, or collective endeavours, there is plenty of scope for action or thinking rooted in the earliest stages of our psychological development.

Rather than pandering to it, psychoanalytically oriented therapy attempts to help us understand and contain our craving for certainty. Of course there is the temptation to beat a horrified retreat from the suffering and disorder of our times to the gratifying comfort of traditional values and answers. The certitudes of one dogmatic faith or another are always available, i.e. the fundamentalism of religion, political ideology, economic doctrine, or even, let it be said, psychological theory. But the apparent safety of '-isms' and a world ordered according to a revelation that has already been handed down masks our susceptibility to the bacillus of violence and repression which is latent in all dogma.

Yet the security contained in allowing ourselves to be consoled in these ways involves a spiritual defeat. It means the defeat of the question by the answer, and requires the submerging of irony, the repressing of ambiguity, and the denial of the sheer relentless complexity of life in favour of a 'final solution': ' … fate has ordained the vicissitudes of shadows and light: the greatest evil comes from those who hold it certain that they are in the light' (Giordano Bruno, burnt by the Inquisition, 1600).

The precarious awareness of the co-existence within us of contradictory impulses and emotions – an awareness which allows us in adult life to tolerate uncertainty, and to celebrate paradox – is a hard-earned, and never securely attained, achievement.

> … More than ever
> life-out-there is goodly, miraculous, loveable,
> but we shan't, not since Stalin and Hitler,
> trust ourselves ever again …
>
> W.H. Auden
> *The Cave of Making*

III

> To us he is no more a person
> now but a whole climate of opinion
>
> W.H. Auden,
> *In Memory Of Sigmund Freud*

Like Copernicus and Darwin, the men with whom he compared himself, Sigmund Freud was a moulder of thought who revolutionized the way we look at ourselves. As the literary critic Harold Bloom has written, Freud's conceptions 'have begun to merge with our culture, and indeed now form the only Western mythology that contemporary intellectuals have in common'.

Yet, psychologically, many devotees of the religious traditions of the West still live in a pre-modern world, with infantile beliefs about God continuing to dominate thinking as if Kant, Kierkegaard and Freud had never existed. Compelled to repeat old ways of thinking, believing and behaving, such religious adherents mythologize and romanticize the past as a way of avoiding the anxieties and demands of the present. Individually or collectively, this 'compulsion to repeat' is, as Freud recognized, a resistance to remembering traumatic pain from the past. But what we end up doing is unconsciously re-enacting that unresolved pain in the present.

Throughout human history there has been a chain of pain and oppression that has been passed from generation to generation. The repetition compulsion that dominates history is the tendency of one generation, recipients of oppression from the past, to act out on the next generation the pain that it experienced.

It is ironical that all three Western monotheistic traditions trace themselves back to Abraham. For it was the revolutionary perception of Abraham that the chain of oppression could be broken. In the story of the binding of Isaac, Abraham is about to do what parents of every generation have done: to express in one form or another their murderous fantasies towards their offspring. The knife is raised and he is about to sacrifice the future because of the ideology of the past – that the gods wish for human sacrifice. But the story dramatizes his recognition that the real voice of God does not want him to sacrifice his child. The power that makes it possible for Abraham to see that the chain of pain and oppression can be broken is what we have called God. This is what makes Abraham the father of all three traditions.

The tragedy of our history is that we have often identified (albeit unconsciously) with the God at the beginning of the narrative who told Abraham to offer up his child, rather than internalizing Abraham's new understanding, gained later in the story, that God is the power which breaks through the received patterns of the past, that God is the power that makes possible the transformation of 'what has always been' into what ought to be.

This points, from a psychological point of view, to a problem at the heart of the monotheistic belief that there is only one God: one God who rules supreme, one God who has done away with the other gods or incorporated them into the Godhead. The problem is that a religious system posited on one supreme being runs the risk of becoming fascistic. Whatever we say about the attributes of our God – that God is the God of love, justice, mercy, compassion and so on – one God means one God *and no others*. The scriptures of the monotheistic faiths are very clear about this. All other gods have to be eliminated. It has to be ensured that the universe is 'cleansed' of other gods – '*Götterrein*', so to speak.

What does it do to people psychologically, to revere a God who cannot tolerate competitors? To love and be in awe of a God who wishes to be the only One? God may love humanity, but he hates other gods. Do we internalize this psychotic split within ourselves and our religious systems? If we are honest we know very well that all our religious ideologies contain within themselves the seeds of intolerance, fanaticism and hatred. All of them can and do murder in the name of a loving God.

Of course the normal defensive response to this is to say, 'But that's not us, that's not "authentic" Judaism, "authentic" Christianity, "authentic" Islam'. I would suggest, however, that it is not good enough to shift the responsibility in this way, to deny that one's own religious tradition or one's own holy literature sanctions fanaticism, hatred and murder. For the sake of our individual and collective psychological health we have to acknowledge the destructive elements in, and potential of, our religious systems; and to also work at transforming those systems.

Part of that transformation involves returning to the central texts of our tradition and learning to re-read them in the light of the new understandings (from whatever source) we have gathered along the way. And this includes – thanks to Freud, and all the diverse schools of practitioners who followed him, arguing and disagreeing with him and each other, yet all committed to the exploration of the psyche – our gradually developing knowledge about unconscious mental processes.

But if we allow this process of re-examination to occur we need to be prepared for some surprises. We might see that the Bible, for example, rather than propounding a clear and unambiguous message, actually defies our innate wish for a world shaped according to a clearly comprehensible story.

The ancient Hebrew writers conveyed the complex moral and psychological realism of their ideas through the art of narrative. But if you convey a people's historical development through fiction this necessitates that the meaning of events is not fixed. One could even suggest that the Hebrew scriptures *aim* to produce an indeterminacy of meaning, particularly in regard to the motives of characters, and their moral and psychological makeup. As the biblical literary scholar Robert Alter has said: 'Meaning was conceived of as a *process* which required continual revision – both in the ordinary sense and in the etymological sense of seeing again'.

To understand the meaning of biblical material requires 'continual suspension of judgement, weighing of multiple possibilities, brooding over gaps in the information provided'. What is distinctive about biblical literature is that conflicting points of view co-exist within it. Events are laid out alongside each other, without comment (just like in life), and we are never allowed to know whether the pattern we see emerging at one point is the true pattern: 'the peculiarity of the Bible is that it keeps calling into question our ability to make sense of our past, and of stories to explain ourselves or describe the world' (Gabriel Josipovici).

It is this stance of 'calling into question' assumptions, certainties, the stories we tell ourselves – and living with the questions – which describes too the task of the therapist.

> Do what you will, this life's a
> fiction
> And is made up of contradiction
>
> William Blake

IV

> The true way leads along a tightrope, which is not stretched aloft but just above the ground. It seems designed more to trip one than to be walked along.
>
> Franz Kafka,
> *Parables and Paradoxes*

IN SPITE of Freud's attempts to outline an objective and scientific model of understanding about the true underlying workings of the human mind, the questions that psychoanalysis asks are not in fact about Truth with a capital T. In relation to religious belief, the artful question asked by the therapist is not 'Is that true?' but 'What in your personal history disposes you to believe that?'

As the psychoanalyst Adam Phillips formulates it: 'From a psychoanalytic point of view belief changes from being a question about the qualities of the object of belief to a question about the history of the subject, the believer. What is the unconscious problem that your belief solves for you or the wishes that it satisfies?' The psychological defences against experiences of helplessness, powerlessness, meaninglessness and despair are many. And we all need some defences against these persecutory feelings. Human needs, desires and fears are manifold and we often look for and create a God to meet our needs and desires or allay our fears.

Some people want a paternal God whom they can look up to and feel protected by; others want a maternal God who would hold and nourish them. In recent years we can see the desire expressed for a return to a potent Goddess with whom one can either identify or in whose immanent presence one can surrender oneself. Whether the divine being we create is one who helps us recreate the security of childhood or one who compensates us for a security which was never enjoyed is not the point here.

What we have to recognize is how deeply we need to feel secure, protected, contained, understood, accepted – and how we search for a God to meet these infantile but also adult needs. But if we create for ourselves – in whatever form we do it – a god image designed to console us and comfort us in the face of our human neediness and fearfulness, then at least we should be aware of and honest about what we are doing.

Psychotherapy does not have to be a substitute for religion, although many people do use it as an alternative source of nurturing as well as a framework for the creation of personal meaning. Psychotherapy can, though, make a crucial contribution to the development of mature religious thinking. An exploration of what in a person's history disposes them towards religious belief can help in the creation of a personal religiosity or spirituality which is not an attempt to solve an unconscious problem or satisfy an infantile wish. The projection of human attributes onto a deity is part of the child's needs within adult thinking. Mature religiosity has to move beyond this.

In doing so we may not be able to keep God good. We may not be able to keep our traditional God at all. An individual may have to discard theistic thinking, just as, within Judaism, animal sacrifices had to be given up once the temple was destroyed. For certain religious concepts and forms become redundant as we make religion subjective and existential. Just as the inwardness of prayer was seen as the natural replacement for the symbolic enactments of the sacrificial system, so the interiorization of the divine can follow our discarding of outmoded models of an external parental God.

If God is not 'out there' any more, if God is not 'factual', but a self-constructed ideal which gives worth to our lives, much of traditional religious doctrinal language becomes redundant. Yet for religious adherents the death of traditional god images need not only be a cause for mourning. As old images are discarded, new images will emerge from the human imagination – as they always have done. As Martin Buber wrote: 'Time after time, the images must be broken, the iconoclasts must have their way … The images topple, but the voice is never silenced …

As we develop, our idea of God will also grow and change; and, as Don Cupitt has suggested, so will the role that idea plays in focusing our aspirations and shaping the course of our lives. Although there may no longer be one overarching, coherent and purposeful outer meaning for human life, creatively alive and evolving god images can perform a vital and healing function in human development. They can help us describe the moral and spiritual goals of our lives – and help us tolerate suffering and the inevitability of death.

The insights of 'secular' psychotherapy can become a spiritual resource when they enable us to take back our projections onto God and recognize in ourselves those qualities we have previously attributed to the deity: our own human capacities for love, goodness, justice, mercy and compassion. We are dependent on these qualities in ourselves and each other. What hinders our human capacities, and this includes our creativity, hinders the 'divine' in us. What helps free ourselves from old, debilitating patterns of behaviour and feeling, what helps develop and deepen our sense of meaning and purpose, whatever therapeutic or other resources we have at our disposal for this work of self-awareness – these become our religious responsibility to use.

The insights we gain can help us too to acknowledge and accept our limitations and our mortality. And with sufficient humility and awareness of paradox, and even a little humour, we may be able to put ourselves centre-stage without becoming as omnipotent as the God we once had.

All of this depends upon our capacity for sustained acts of interpretation in the spirit of what John Keats called 'negative capability': when a person 'is capable of being in uncertainties, mysteries, doubts, without any irritable reaching after fact and reason …'. At their best, both the religious and therapeutic stances acknowledge the liberating energy embodied in this interpretative attitude. Whether the texts interpreted are written, or inscribed in the heart and memory of the individual, interpretation is the key to our survival: for interpretation is polymorphous, and that means that our lives, as with every work of art, are beyond analysis, relentless with meaning and resistant to the totalitarianism of certainty.

> For me, the notion of some complete and finite knowledge, that explains everything and raises no further questions, relates clearly to the end of an idea – an end to the spirit, to life, to time and to being. However, anything meaningful ever said on the matter (including every religious gospel) is remarkable for its dramatic openness, its incompleteness. It is not a conclusive statement so much as a challenge or an appeal … which never, of course, attempts to settle unequivocally the unanswerable question of meaning. Instead it tends to suggest how to live with the question.
>
> Vaclav Havel,
Letters from Prison, 1981

Bibliography

ALTER, ROBERT, *The Art of Biblical Narrative* (New York, Basic Books, 1981)

BETTELHEIM, BRUNO, *Freud and Man's Soul* (London, Fontana Paperbacks, 1982)

COLTART, NINA, *Slouching Towards Bethlehem … And Further Psychoanalytic Explorations* (London, Free Association Books, 1992)

CUPITT, DON, *The Sea of Faith* (London, BBC Books, 1984)

GAY, PETER, *Freud: A Life for Our Time* (London, J.M. Dent & Sons, 1984)

HAVEL, VACLAV, 'Letters From Prison', in *Granta* 21

HOBSON, ROBERT, *Forms of Feeling: The Heart of Psychotherapy* (Tavistock Publications, 1985)

JOSIPOVICI, GABRIEL, *The Book of God* (Yale, Yale University Press, 1988)

LERNER, MICHAEL, *Jewish Renewal: A Path to Healing and Transformation* (Harper Collins, 1995)

PHILLIPS, ADAM, *On Kissing, Tickling and Being Bored* (London, Faber and Faber, 1993)

RYCROFT, CHARLES, *Psychoanalysis and Beyond* (London, Chatto & Windus, 1985)

RUSHDIE, SALMAN, *Imaginary Homelands: Essays and Criticism 1981–1991* (Oxford, Granta Books, 1991)

– 9 –

THE STATE AND SOCIETY
A Relationship Balanced to Prevent Both Hegemony and Degeneration

Mohammad Abdul Jabbar is the author of *The Future of Democracy in Iraq* (1994), *The Theory of Society in Qu'ran* (1984), *The Islamic Civilization* (1991) and other books as wells as many essays in arabic newspapers and magazines. He was the editor-in-chief of *Al-Jihad* weekly (Tehran 1981–1983) *Al-Badeel Al-Islami* weekly (Beirut 1986–1992) and is editor-in-chief of *Al-Mutamar* weekly (London).

MOHAMMAD ABDUL JABBAR

Introduction

THE STUDY of the relationship between the state and society from an Islamic point of view is fraught with theoretical and practical difficulties. From a theoretical standpoint, neither the Holy Qu'rān nor the Prophet's Sunna, being the two essential texts in Islam, offer a ready-made model for this question. These two holy texts are characteristically lacking in theories, since their main concern is the presentation of essential, practical guidance to Muslims contemporary to the prophet's mission. This also applies to politics, faith, social interaction, theology, economics etc. When the need arose for the formulation of theories, whether in theology as required in earlier periods or the social sciences as required in more recent times, Muslim theoreticians had to re-read these texts in search of answers to these new questions. This research into theoretics rather than dogma ran into numerous difficulties because of the lack of relevant texts. These problems were partially solved by Imam Sayed Mohammed Baqir Al-Sadr through his pathfinding attempt to discover an Islamic Economic Theory in the texts of the Qu'rān and the Sunna and in the opinions of the theologians who preceded him.

One difficulty is the fact that Islamic states have emerged since the death of the Prophet Mohammed in 10 AH. These states differ in the extent of their embodiment of what may be considered as an Islamic theory relating government to society. These differences arose from conditions prevalent at the time of the emergence of these states. Furthermore, human understanding of scripture and law differed as a result of differing conditions as well as personality factors. This is exemplified on the one hand by a ruler whose concern is primarily with governing, as was the case with the first four Caliphs (10–40 AH), and on the other hand by the theologian who is concerned primarily with understanding. The differentiation between the two has become more pronounced in recent times. There have been recent calls for the consolidation of the two attitudes: concern with government and concern with religious knowledge and theology, as in the Theological Ruler (in Arabic: Willayat Al Faqeih) theory. Some have considered these practical applications, especially those of the first four Caliphs, as precedents and having the same legislative power as the Qu'rān and the Sunna. Others, however, see them as human experiments permitted to Muslims under Islam within what is known theologically as 'the empty area in Islamic law'. This is the area left to nations, rulers and theologians to fill in accordance with contemporary needs. This has become a matter of contention among the various factions and thinkers.

This search also requires the study of the meaning of the terms: state, political society and civil society in Islamic texts and thought. These terms are not present in the Qu'rān or the Sunna or authoritative interpretations. However, these sources reveal expressions which are similar in meaning.

The Need for the State

The development of an Islamic view of the relationship between the state and the individual has become an important issue ever since there has been a growing concern with human rights. Appropriate safeguards are sought to protect the citizen from state pressure and harassment. This subject is still uncharted territory in Islamic thought and requires exploration. No one can deny the need for a state even if government is not possible without compromise and the evil consequences. The Marxist predictions of the demise of the state have proved to be Utopian dreams. Seventy years after the creation of the Marxist state, the importance of government did not diminish. In fact, the opposite happened: the state overwhelmed the life of every individual, and left him no personal freedom in the world of thought or action. We now know, from historical experience as well as from theoretical analysis, that Engels was wrong when he said:

> ... the state will necessarily cease to exist: the society which organizes production in the new way based on uniting the producers freely and equally, shall send the entire mechanism of government to where it then shall belong: to the museum, alongside the primitive spinning spindle and the bronze ax.[1]

By contrast, Imam Ali's statement 'People need an Emir' has been shown to be true as has the quote from Imam AlSadiq: 'People will not be improved except by an Imam.' Government is necessary to human societies. The late Mohammed Hussain AlTabatabai said:

> Human society cannot do without this position, and I mean the position of King (= ruler or government) regardless of any changes in designation or trappings in different nations or with the passage of time.[2]

All the Muslim factions agree upon this statement except the Najdat [Bin Amer AlHanafi] who said that people do not need an Imam i.e. a state at all, that people should be fair amongst themselves, but if they found that this could not be achieved without an Imam, they instated one!

It is true that the state did not appear simultaneously with the appearance of mankind. It had hardly appeared prior to recorded history, as Durant writes in his book *The Story of Civilization*, but quickly became 'an irreplaceable pillar of order' since 'it is not only a force for order, but also reconciles the interests of hundreds of conflicting groups which comprise society in its complex form.'

While the Marxist theory of the state's decline has been proven wrong, the capitalist theory of a limited role for the state has also receded.

> We find that the state in the capitalist society has begun to play a direct role in supervising production activity, since the state in most of these societies utilizes about 40% of the work

1 Engels, *Origin of Family*, Arabic edition, Moscow, p. 230.
2 Mohammad Hussein Al Tabatabai, *Almizan*, vol 3, p. 146.

force, either in its administrative structure or in its national industries. The state is also attempting to interfere in economic activity by trying to influence the supply and demand for goods, as well as in economic planning and in price and income policies. This is in addition to the increasing role of the state in the other aspects of social life, especially in what is known as the affluent society, and the positive role of the state in providing the services required by this society.[3]

Dr Fuad Mursi was not wrong in saying: 'There is no capitalist state today that does not subscribe to centralized planning, to one degree or another.'

It is known that both classical and contemporary Islamic thinking have given the state a major role in the life of society. AlMawardi listed 'ten things' of public affairs which are required to be undertaken by the Caliph who must consider them as rights of the 'nation'. These are the preservation of the religion, the execution of the law, the providing of security, the implementation of sentences, the reinforcement of weaknesses, the Jihad for the sake of Islam, the collection of taxes, the estimation of contributions, the employment of fiduciaries, and lastly the undertaking of matters himself.

The Islamic peoples in particular, and third world peoples in general, suffer from the excesses of their rulers, which is in dramatic contrast to their demand for 'salvation' from their dictator. This coincides with the growth of the worldwide popular struggle to reclaim freedom from tyrannical rulers and to convert to democratic systems which respect human rights. This has been taking place since the collapse of the Soviet Union and the Iron Curtain.

No longer are the Islamic movements merely forces for struggle with governments, nor are they only religious forces resisting deviation. Rather, they have become political forces with agendas for government. In some countries, they have already achieved this position. In other countries they are still aspiring to it by revolution or have taken part in political life to achieve their end within the existing legal framework. Whether these movements demand an Islamic state or a secular state, it has become incumbent upon them to actively participate in the worldwide shift toward freedom, democracy, and human rights. This is pursued both on a practical level through daily efforts, and on a theoretical level through the presentation of ideas that contribute to a constructive relationship between the state and society which precludes the tyranny of the state and the deprivation of individual rights.

The Islamic movement, which enjoys an undeniable effect on the Arab and Islamic masses, bears a special responsibility to enlighten these masses with regard to their political and human rights. It must work to free them of the 'chains' of dictatorial abuse, and of the systematic official violation of their rights at the hands of the regimes which disguise themselves as Islamic and as proponents of human

---

3 Fuad Mursi, *Al Ra'asmalia Tujadid Nafsaha*, p. 196.

rights. This is in accordance with the words of the Almighty:

> ... those who shall follow the (last) Apostle, the unlettered Prophet whom they shall find described in the Torah that is with them, and (later on) in the Gospel: (the prophet) who will enjoin upon them the doing of what is right and forbid them the doing of what is wrong, and make lawful to them the good things of life and forbid them the bad things, and lift from them their burdens and the shackles that were upon them. (AL-ARAF 157)

Discussion today is not about the need for a state; it is rather about the means of regulating the relationship between the state and the civilian population. This is in view of the suffering of many peoples, the Arabic and Islamic peoples among them, caused by the inordinate growth of the state and its tyranny – a situation which has made the quest for democracy a worldwide demand. This is where an Islamic view of this relationship must be sought, a view which embodies the Islamic values that revolve around mankind and his place on earth, since he is God's inheritor of His earth. This means that the relationship between the state and the civilian population must consider the individual, including his position, his rights, his role in society and the state as a supreme value; individual's rights should be the object of any proposed relationship, to be guarded and entrenched, and protected from any form of state abuse, in keeping with Qu'rānic texts, one of which says: 'We have conferred dignity on the children of Adam.' (AL-ISRA)

The Qu'rānic Basis for the Relationship between State and Society
An Islamic concept of the relationship between the state and society in Islamic theory must be inferred from the Islamic view of the three-way relationship between God, society, and the state, based on the following triangle:

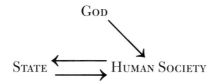

This triangle produces three relationship axes, which are:

1 The relationship between God and human society. [one arrow]
2 The relationship between God and the state. [no arrow]
3 The relationship between human society and the state. [two arrows]

In the *First Axis*, there is one arrow between the two sides of the relationship which are God and human society, noting that the direction of the arrow is from God to human society which means that, in this case, the relationship is one-sided. Direction comes from God.

The Holy Qu'rān offers the following basic criteria for the relationship between God and human society:

- creation
- successorship
- guidance
- no coercion in matters of faith
- punishment and recompense

God is the creator of the universe and humanity. This relationship gives God certain rights over mankind, covered by the two words: 'sovereignty' and 'possession', meaning the right of disposition. God has total authority over mankind. There are two kinds of authority: that of the creator, and the authority of His legislation.

However God did not choose to utilize His full authority as the creator. Rather, He made mankind His successor on earth: 'Your Sustainer said unto the angels: Behold, I am about to establish upon earth one who shall inherit it.' (AL-BAQARAH) This means that God placed mankind there in His stead. He thus delegated the authority not of creation but of legislation to mankind. This second authority is limited to those areas which He left empty for mankind to fill.

The concept of 'successorship' forms the cornerstone of the Islamic understanding of the elements of society, and its relationship with God through this concept. The martyred Imam Sayed Mohammed Baqir Al-Sadr considered the successorship relationship to be the basis for government:

> God delegated Mankind to rule and lead the Universe, and to develop it socially and naturally; it is on this basis that we have the theory of people ruling themselves, and the legality of Mankind ruling themselves, being the Successors to God.

In order for man to fulfil his role of successor on earth, God has taken responsibility for his spiritual salvation by showing him the way forward with ideas, beliefs, and religious rules. Reaching the goal is humanity's responsibility. 'We have shown him (man) the way: (and it rests with him to prove himself) either grateful or ungrateful.' (AL-INSAN 3)

Guidance is based on another pillar of the relationship between man and God, that there is no compulsion by force. 'There shall be no coercion in matters of faith.' (AL-BAQARAH 256) Man has freedom of choice, even though he is a creature of God and has been deemed by Him as His successor on earth. God does not force man to follow the path of salvation which He has shown him. Neither do the prophets sent by God to deliver His message of salvation have the authority to force people to obey God's message. The matter is left to man's faith and to his free and responsible choice: 'And had your Sustainer so willed, all those who live on earth would surely have attained to faith, all of them: do you, then, think that you could compel people to believe?' (YUNUS 99)

This is the justification for the final criterion in the relationship between God and human society: 'punishment and recompense'. God, while relinquishing His right to enforce submission, has still retained the right to punish man if he chooses a path other than that of salvation, or to reward him if he follows it. 'It is in no wise for you (O Prophet) to decide whether He shall accept their repentance or chastise them.' (AL-IMRAN 128)

If we now look at the *Second Axis* of the relationship, that between mankind and the state, what do we find? Firstly we find that the state (the body which enforces the rule of law) is a necessity required by human society. Secondly, since the state is a necessity, it is natural that God should teach His prophets the correct way of constructing it. This teaching falls under that of 'salvation', one of the elements of the relationship between God and mankind. Thus it can be said that the state has a prophetic element. God has shown people that a healthy state is one that operates in accordance with divine salvation: 'Yet if people of those communities had but attained to faith and been conscious of Us, We would indeed have opened up for them blessings out of heaven and earth.'(AL-ARAF) Man makes the state, good or bad. By behaving properly, he can preserve it, and by his improper behaviour, he will cause its collapse. It is thus a human phenomenon. Mohammed Taqi AlNabhani says: 'It is a human political state, it is neither spiritual nor divine, it has no sanctity, nor does its leader possess the attribute of infallibility.' Thirdly, the state has enormous influence over people, since it is the most powerful component of society. However, the state's effect on its society is not total. It too is affected by its populace. That is why it has also been said that your rulers are a reflection of yourselves. Thus, the relationship between the state and society is mutually influential. Finally, authority remains with the populace who make up the state, since they are the successors of God on earth, and any form of rule which confiscates this right is rejected by Islam.

Considering the *Third Axis* in the relationship, we find that there is no direct relationship between God and the state. God does not make the state, nor does He rule it directly. He does not appoint its leader, nor does He protect it from collapsing if it falls victim to internal conflicts. Thus, the state of the first four Caliphs fell, as did other Islamic states. The state is a human, and not a divine entity, nor does its ruler have a divine mandate. 'God has not devolved His authority to any of His creatures', says the Imam AlSadiq Ja'far Bin Mohammed. This is not in conflict with the opinion that the state is a prophetic phenomenon, because while it has been brought about by the efforts of the prophets it is not imbued with divine attributes.

Two Forms of the Relationship between the State and Society
Human experience has produced two levels of this relationship: firstly, one in which the state has supremacy over society and secondly, one in which society has supremacy over the state. After ascertaining the continued existence of this evil known as the state, we are concerned with limiting the authority of the state to the point

where it can no longer overwhelm its society, nor persecute its citizens. Dictatorial regimes create states that dominate their societies, turning their citizens into individuals without effective personalities, thus assuming guardianship over society, whether the authority of such a state is in the form of a ruling party, a military junta, or an authoritarian individual. Often the first two kinds of relationships devolve into the third, with the usurping of the reins of power by an individual who transforms it into a source of personal enjoyment, or into a personified autocracy which he uses at his whim, without the need for him to render any accountability or to follow any binding principles. History has shown painful examples of such a transformation, most notorious of such individual dictatorships being those of Hitler, Stalin, and Saddam. It is these bitter examples that strike fear into those who aspire to a life free of enslavement and persecution.

Larry Diamond, author of *The Democratic Revolution*, says that the tendency of the state is to impose its maximum authority over society. It is known that the state achieves this by monopolizing military power, creating an army and a police force, levying taxes, regulating the economy and commerce and industry, imposing censorship on the newspapers and the media, and controlling educational institutions and faculties. He adds that a totalitarian state is distinguished by its abolition of civilian society, prostrating all forms of expression and glorification to the control of the state and party driving its affairs. This is one of the characteristics of totalitarian regimes as defined by Raymond Aaron, others being the monopolization of political activity, and the imposition of official ideology as mentioned by Alain Touraine.

The Qu'rān has discussed such regimes using the term 'pharaonic', and we can also use this designation to describe totalitarian and dictatorial regimes, if we wish to use Qu'rānic terminology in our modern political literature. In their valuable study, *The Sociology of the State*, Bertrand Bady and Pierre Bierenbaum offer France as an example of the state being victorious over society, and Britain as an example of the opposite.

The situation in which society overwhelms the state is not an ideal one, since it is also fraught with danger and must be avoided. Imam Ali said, 'If the state should lose its grandeur in society, it would also lose its ability to carry out its functions. The various groupings that make up society may not, in such an event, be able to retain cohesion; society would disintegrate and the state would collapse.' This is what happened in Lebanon, when the local groupings and branch organizations grew in power within society, and exceeded the power of the state which became unable to impose its will or to fulfil its traditional functions. What is required is a balanced relationship which limits the authority of the state, preventing it from becoming authoritarian over society, while permitting both the state and society the performance of their functions in a proper way.

The Balanced Relationship

Imam Ali drew a picture of the balanced relationship between the state and society, in saying:

> The greatest of the rights promulgated by God is the right of the ruler on his constituents, and the right of the constituents on their ruler, a requirement imposed by God on each for each, making it an orderliness in their harmony, an uplifting of their religion, for the dependents cannot be redeemed without the redemption of the rulers, and rulers cannot be redeemed without correctness in the dependents, for if the dependents fulfilled the ruler's right and the ruler fulfilled his dependents' right, then propriety will have been established between them, the programs of religion will have been erected, justice will have prevailed, behavioural precedents will have flowed their proper way, the era will have been redeemed, people would aspire to the continuance of the state, and the enemies' greed will have been rendered hopeless. But if the dependents overcame their ruler, or if the ruler were unjust to his dependents, there would be divergences of opinion, the signs of tyranny would appear, impurities would contaminate the Religion, and the following of precedents would be abandoned. Then activity would be governed by whim, legislation would break down, and there would be an increase in the ills of souls.[4]

According to this text, both the ruler, the state and the citizens must behave properly, and the relationship between them must be established on the basis of a bill of mutual rights and obligations. Discussion here will revolve around the means of bringing about such a positive relationship. Islamic texts are united in their understanding of the proper state. There are two criteria to measure a state's propriety; one which considers a state to be proper if it implements Islamic law, the other deems a state proper if it ensures justice among its people. A direct relationship exists between the first and second criteria, since the implementation of Islamic law requires justice among people as specified by its laws. But this convergence is dependent upon the proper implementation of Islamic law. One can also assume an inverted divergence, that is one can visualize the provision of justice among the people even without the implementation of Islamic law. This was not far from Ibn Khaldun's mind when he differentiated between political rule and the Caliphate, defining the first as: 'requiring everyone to seek the requirements of securing worldly benefits and avoiding harm's way'. He defined the Caliphate as: 'requiring everyone to seek the requirements of the *Sharia* in aspiring to their after-life interests and the worldly interests related to them.'

The Islamic state was on the way to achieving this balanced relationship during the era of the first four Caliphs. With some exceptions, it was rich in innovative and constructive words and deeds in this field; unfortunately, it suffered reversals which resulted in the acquisition of absolute power by the Omayad Caliphs. The power of the Caliph took on the form of rule associated with the Divine Mandate theory which was widely known in Europe. With the degradation of the Caliphate's

---

4 Imam Ali, *Nahj ul Balaga*, pp. 333–4.

true authority, absolute power was transferred to the military leaders and local princes, who not only achieved total control over political power, but also a sentient split between themselves and their dependents. This has had the most profound effect on the negative development of the relationship between the state and society in Islamic and Arabic political life at the present time.

The question occupying the minds of political analysts and proponents of democracy and human rights is how to limit the power of the state. This essay's objective is to generate thought about the matter in an attempt to reach a consensus view of social, political, and civilian activity which can be a basis for achieving a harmonious relationship between the state and the society it rules. It would be legitimate here to ponder what Islam can offer. We have seen that Islam calls for a balanced relationship between the state and civilian society. This balanced relationship presumes the existence of a balance of power between the two, and a precise delineation of the authority of each, preventing the infliction of damage on one side by the other in general, and such infliction by the state on society in particular, in view of the state's capability of overwhelming society.

It seems that the Islamic view of this dilemma is founded on two axes: firstly, the establishment of limits and restrictions on the authority of the state, and secondly, the strengthening of civilian society to enable it to withstand the pressures and impositions of the state. We can make the following observations on the *First Axis:* firstly, Islam confirms the human character of the state, and that it does not have a divine mandate. This is to prevent tyranny being perpetrated in the name of God; secondly, defining the authority of the state in a written constitution. It is alien to Islam to found a state with absolute power over society. Absolute power leads to tyranny, in contradiction with the spirit of Islam and its general intentions. The scholar Mohammed Hussain AlTabatabai says:

> Islam, imbued as it is with the spirit of upholding Good and decrying Evil, will not permit the rule of despots pretending decency; nor will it permit silence and the patient acceptance of suffering and persecution, at the hands of tyrants and those who are corrupt, by those who aspire to the righting of wrongs.[5]

The written constitution is the body of Islamic law (*Sharia*) or what is derived from it by an Islamic state; or it is the secular constitution in the case of a non-Islamic state. The constitution is the ruler of both the state and society. The Holy Qu'rān forcefully warns of this in many of its verses which decry those who do not rule in accordance with God's revelations (i.e. the written constitution). Thus, an Islamic authority, or any other authority with which Islam and Islamicists can coexist, must be an administrative authority based on laws and not that of an individual. Authoritarian individuals, however, behave as if the matter is related to their

---

5 Mohammad Hussein Al Tabatabai, *Almizan*, vol 15, p. 158.

personal private property, to be used or abused at will. An autocrat's will is the unrestricted law and his followers are bound by personal allegiances. Thus it becomes total tyranny.

Thirdly, the state must be subject to the choices of the nation. As the Islamic state acquires its religious justifiability by adhering to the Islamic *Sharia*, so it acquires its political justifiability from the allegiance of the nation. This differentiation between the two is necessary. People do not grant religious legality to anybody, nor do they withhold it from him, because the matter is linked to the adherence of the individual, or group, or the state to the dictates of Islam. According to Islamic religious measurement, he who is committed to them is on the right path. But personal commitment does not ensure the automatic granting of political authority over people, unless it is authorized by them. The religious expert (as designated by his followers), or an Islamic party, or any individual or group aspiring to power, is merely a nominee who must seek the support of the people for his nomination. At present, this is achieved through elections. This has its origin in the principle that the individual is master of himself and what is his, and the principle of the 'divine successorship of mankind' which we mentioned earlier. Based on this, there can be no exercise of power over people without their acceptance, their agreement, and their authorization, i.e. their granting of allegiance, i.e. their commitment to 'the promise of obedience'.

Imam Ali said: 'Your affairs are nobody else's affairs, except him whom you have chosen.' The origin of the granting of allegiance is fixed in the Holy Qu'rān. There are broad options available to the nation and civilian society in this regard, even within the confines of the *Sharia*. Imam AlSadr discussed this question in detail and has shown that the nation's adherence to the *Sharia* is to be achieved as follows:

1. The nation adheres to the dictates of the *Sharia* clearly and unequivocally, and considers it, in as far as it applies to social life, to be an integral part of the constitution.

2. The nation selects that which it considers appropriate to the common good, from among the numerous theological opinions on the unified position.

3. The legislative authority representing the nation promulgates whatever laws it deems appropriate in the absence of a definitive position in the *Sharia*, regarding forbidding or permitting.[6]

Since the state is the stronger side in this state-society equation, it is necessary to work towards strengthening civilian society in the face of the power of the state to over-run it. Civilian society is the area in which the various social groupings

---

6 Imam Al-Sadr, *Al Islam Yaqud Alhayat*, p. 18–19.

operate, such as neighbourhood leagues, women's organizations, cultural trends and civilian organizations of all classes. This is in contrast to political society, the realm of politicians and administrations, in which there is competition for the control of the state. Larry Diamond says:

> A strong civilian society is capable of contributing to the strengthening of democracy by various means ... since it represents a vast reservoir of resources – political, economic, cultural, and moral – to calibrate and correct the state. It includes a powerful number of independent unions and the media: the foundation for limiting the power of the state, the eventual control of the state by society, and hence the democratic political organizations which are the most effective means to exert such control. When the state controls the media, there is no longer a means of exposing its weaknesses or the corruption within it ... the presence of a large number of factions noisily insisting on their rights and cleverly presenting their interests prevents the state from succumbing to a particular faction, and forces the state to be answerable to its citizens and to respond to their demands and concerns ... This does not depend only on the strength of civilian society, but also on its variety and diversity.[7]

On the Islamic level, we find that Islam strives to strengthen civilian society in a large number of ways, of which we can list a few as follows: Firstly, Islam praises the strong individual and the strong nation (the active self, in Tureen's words) in the face of the ruler or the state; it cautions against blind submission and abject surrender to a tyrannical state, rather it calls for resisting it. Secondly, the Qu'rān encourages the creation of civilian organizations external to the authority of the state. Among them is the 'Organization for Demanding Good and Decrying Evil' and the 'Organization of Theological Experts' both of whom we referred to at the beginning of this article. There is nothing in Islam which prohibits the creation of similarly-inclined organizations. We can assume that the Qu'rānic verse: 'Help one another in furthering virtue and God-consciousness' (ALMAIDA 2) incorporates an open invitation to create civilian organizations, unions, and co-operatives, related to the needs of society and its degree of development – the existence of these organizations expresses the strength of presence of civilian society.

---

7 Diamond, Larry, *The Democratic Revolution*, (Arabic Edition), p. 17.

– 10 –

RELIGION, SECULARISM AND WOMEN

Julia Neuberger became a rabbi in 1977, and served the South London Liberal Synagogue for twelve years, before going to the Kings Fund Institute as a Visiting Fellow, to work on research ethics committees in the United Kingdom. She then became a fellow at Harvard Medical School in 1991–2 and became Chairman of Camden and Islington Community Health Service NHS Trust in April 1993. She holds honorary doctorates from seven universities and has been Chancellor of the University of Ulster since 1994. She is also the author of several books on women, on healthcare ethics and on caring for dying people. Her book *On Being Jewish* was published in 1995. She broadcasts frequently, and writes articles on a variety of subjects.

JULIA NEUBERGER

RELIGIONS the world over have not, on the whole, offered equal opportunities to women. In many religious systems, women are second-class citizens, their roles clearly defined and their lives seriously circumscribed. The nature of their religious longings, or of their spirituality, has frequently been left to one side, whilst men discuss the more important theological issues about angels on the heads of pins or whether an inadvertent lump of butter, less than one sixtieth of the volume of the chicken, can be ignored when cooked with the chicken, or whether it renders the whole dish non-kosher. Of such debates, to lampoon only gently, is male theological discussion made.

Obviously that is not wholly true. But there is, without doubt, a conscious denigration of women in many of our religious faiths to this very day. The debate about the ordination of women in the Church of England, which thankfully resulted in women's ordination to the priesthood from 1994 onwards, illustrated that low image of women all too clearly. A previous Bishop of London, Dr Graham Leonard, argued that seeing a woman in the pulpit would make him wish to take her in his arms. An Anglican curate, interviewed in the *Independent* (23 February 1987), said that 'you might as well ordain a pot of anchovy paste as a woman'. Meanwhile, using theoretically theological arguments, some argued that Jesus had not had female disciples, and therefore a priest could not be female. Or, worse, listening to the voice of Paul on the subject of Eve's sin:

> A woman must be a learner, listening quietly and with due submission. I do not permit a woman to be a teacher, nor must women dominate over man; she should be quiet. For Adam was created first and then Eve; and it was not Adam who was deceived; it was the woman, who yielding to deception, fell into sin. (1 *Timothy* 2:11–14)

Similarly, in the recent report of the commission on the position of women in Anglo-Jewry set up by Chief Rabbi Dr Jonathan Sacks, a large number of questions are left unanswered, and it emerges that Dr Sacks himself put the dampers on several conclusions, so that no immediate action to encourage women into religious observance would be allowed (*Jewish Chronicle* 8 July 1994). There is no active encouragement of women-only using the Torah scroll (scroll of the Law), even though there is no theological objection. And there is no will to look at the services and re-establish a women's liturgy, particularly relating to childbirth and to a girl's maturation at twelve (the traditional age in Judaism), so that the girl might be allowed to conduct the service and read from the scroll in the same way as the boys do at Bar Mitzvah. All these things could fit within traditional Judaism, and require none of the radical rethink of Reform and Liberal Judaism at all, with their abandonment of the traditional liturgy in the morning service where a man thanks God for not making him a woman and the woman simply thanks God for making her as she is. Though apologists argue that this is said because men have to perform all the religious duties for which there is a fixed time, and they are delighted to carry out God's will, whilst women are exempt, the reply to that has to be that women did not ask to be exempt and indeed are now largely excluded, which is clearly not for their benefit.

There are hundreds of examples of quotations from the religious texts of Judaism, Christianity and Islam which are less than favourable to women, and often deliberately denigratory. It demonstrates, of course, a serious state of affairs. It is as if to say that organized religion is the province of men, that women are useful only to make the tea, that the fun, spiritual highs, official recognition and so on are all for the boys. Women, Keep out! Beware …

There is no doubt that the major structures of Judaism, Christianity and Islam were developed by men. The major structures of Judaism were developed between roughly 200 BCE and 500 CE, with the development of the legal codes out of much earlier legal material. We can date the Mishnah, the first codification of the Law, to about 200 CE and the Babylonian Talmud, the development of the Mishnah with commentary and legal debate, to about 500 CE, in the course of which few women are mentioned and even fewer given credit. There are exceptions, such as Beruriah, wife of the famous Rabbi Meir, who was reputed to be wiser than he, but they are very few. Meanwhile a considerable amount of attention is given to matters sexual, all from the male point of view, (for women do not enter the debate, although they have sexual rights) and to matters of ritual impurity, particularly concerned with menstruation and childbirth. Yet no women, as far as we know, ever joined the debate to speak from personal experience.

Similarly in Christianity. Though we know that there were women followers of Jesus, and the stories of Mary Magdalene and Martha lend weight to that assumption, women became chattels, possessions of their husbands, rather than free-standing people. Though we know that the early Church had many women involved, much of what was said to them was about their insuperable evil, or vanity, or whatever. In Peter Brown's magnificent work on attitudes to the body in the early Church,[1] he makes it clear that in order to be accepted as part of the community, as a follower or whatever, a woman had to make herself disgusting, be filthy, wear appalling clothes, and ignore her appearance. Such an attitude in itself suggests a strange attitude to women, and to sexuality, a case made strongly by Karen Armstrong in *The Gospel according to Woman*.[2]

Yet Christianity, unlike Judaism and Islam, (which has similar restrictions on women to those of Judaism, but has in recent years, particularly in some fundamentalist regimes, moved towards a far stricter attitude to modesty and restriction away from public life) created a religious role for women. What it has, which in some

---

1   Peter Brown, *The Body and Society – Man, Women and Sexual Renunciation in Early Christianity* (Faber, London 1989).

2   Karen Armstrong, *The Gospel According to Woman* (Elm Tree, London, 1986).

ways is central to Christian thinking when one looks at it from the outside, is a dichotomy. The woman can either be a sexual being, have children, wear attractive clothes, be concerned with matters of vanity, be dirty (with menstrual blood and so on) and live an earthly, inferior life (inferior to men as well as to the religious life) as a chattel of some other person, usually male. Or she can enter the spiritual life, spend her days in prayer and contemplation, in an order consisting only of women, and thereby earn religious respect and satisfy her religious and spiritual longings, if not her physical ones. It is an either/or situation. But at least, sequestered from the attentions of importuning males, she has the chance to do something religious. In Judaism and Islam, she has no such chance, and must accept her lot as a lower being, though never as low a being as the status her Christian sisters who did not opt for the conventual life would have experienced. Not for nothing do we read rhymes from seventeenth- and eighteenth-century Europe about the value of a wife compared with that of a cow:[3]

> If the cow kicks off, mighty cross.
> If the wife kicks off, no big loss. (Hesse)

or:

> Got a dead wife? No big deal.
> Got a dead horse? How you squeal. (Franconia)

Examining attitudes such as these, and realizing they were the predominant attitudes in Europe for probably a millennium or more, leads one to ask why it is that religion, apparently the purveyor of all right and true thinking, never questioned such a state of affairs. Why was it in Judaism, for instance, that the position of women was allowed to diminish from a period when women were exempt from performing religious duties (*mitzvot*) for which there was a set time, presumably because of domestic duties, to one where that exemption became an exclusion? Why was it that no-one apparently asked the question about the role of women who were not overburdened by children and domestic duties, the women who never married, for instance, whose lot was said to be a sorry one, or women who were childless (in which case they could be divorced in favour of another wife for their husband, so that he could fulfil the commandment, which applies to men and not to women[!], of being fruitful and multiplying), or the rare women who had had their families, had survived multiple childbirth, and were now relatively free agents? It seems odd that these questions were apparently never asked, or, if asked, never recorded. It seems even odder that only now are these questions being asked (and resisted by religious establishments) with the advent of feminism, a brand of thinking which is

---

3 Taken from Edward Shorter: *A History of Women's Bodies* (London, 1983) who takes this saying from Adolf Mueller: *Beitraege hessischen Medizingeschichte des 15–18 Jahrhunderts* (Darmstadt, 1929) and Ludwig Buettner: *Fraenkische Volksmedizin* (Erlangen, 1935).

not necessarily a belief pattern in itself, but which has its roots in eighteenth-century rationalism, and in rights-based thinking of the late-eighteenth and early-nineteenth centuries. There are some who would argue that its roots go back earlier, to the Puritan leveller tradition and to a Christian view, but insofar as such thinking affected women, it is the eighteenth century which is significant.

For in that century Mary Wollstonecraft wrote her *Vindication of the Rights of Women*. Women began to be poets, novelists and to blossom beyond the domestic role. There began to be talk about the education of girls, as salons were established by educated, witty and intelligent women in the great cities of Europe, women for whom showing intelligence was an art and to be cultivated rather than a disadvantage to be disguised.

The nineteenth century brought the campaign for girls' education, the establishment of girls' schools, the gradual beginnings of the suffragist movement, and role of women as social reformers. Women began to have a role outside the family, other than in the domestic service role if poor and in governess role if genteel. The writing tradition grew. Women wrote novels and plays and poems, at the beginning of the century under assumed male names, but by the end of the century under their own names, and Queen Victoria was at least a titular female role model.

But on the whole religion did not keep up. Women kept silent in the churches. Religion was popular. It was regarded as a strange thing indeed not to attend church or synagogue. But women played no real part. Yet with the emancipation of the Jews in Germany, and the rise of the early reform movement in Judaism, there was a shift. People began to talk about the education of girls. The Reverend D.W. Marks, in his consecration sermon at the West London Synagogue, Britain's first reform synagogue, in 1842, raised the issue of the education of girls and poured scorn on the idea that one could possibly educate children without their mothers being educated Jewishly as well. In Germany, girls were confirmed (a later version of Bar Mitzvah) as well as boys in the early Reform synagogue at Seesen. In the United States, women began to sit with the men rather than in the ladies' gallery, and the beginnings of a change came about.

But not in mainstream orthodoxy. A similar pattern can be traced in some varieties of nonconformist Christianity. There were female ministers in the Congregational Church (now part of the United Reformed Church) from the 1920s. But the Roman Catholic church showed no signs of change, and neither did the Church of England until comparatively recently. There was an almost deliberate relishing of social conservatism. Images of elderly ladies arranging flowers, and the discreet passions of women for their vicars, as evidenced in the novels of Barbara Pym, were what it all seemed to be about, as Cathedral closes basked in the sun and cucumber sandwiches were served for tea. The Church of England seemed inescapably caught up with class and a social conservatism. The Roman Catholic church was less grand in most cases, but even more socially conservative, with its attitudes to contraception and abortion alienating many women. And the Jewish community continued to take its low-key tone from the churches, to maintain a dominant conservatism (unlike the United States, where non-orthodox Judaism of one sort or another is dominant over orthodoxy). Women remained excluded. Yet all the evidence has shown that young girls have stronger religious feelings than young boys, and in the Christian churches it is usually the case that women outnumber the men in church attendance. (The same is not true in Judaism and Islam where women are not traditionally perceived as 'necessary' to conduct a full service.)

It is therefore no surprise that women often feel alienated, which is not to say that many women are not content with the innate conservatism of most religious organisations. The rise of feminism has made many women, including the least radical imaginable, question the *status quo*. And, in religious organizations, the *status quo* is not up to much for women. Feminism requires that women have equal opportunities, a position adopted by non-orthodox Judaism in the last century but nowhere near true in practice. Feminism demands that the world be looked at through women's eyes. A glancing scan of much religious literature from a women's point of view begs a huge number of questions. Why does Judaism rate the patriarchs, a pretty appalling bunch of people if truth be told, over the matriarchs? Why are women ritually impure for seven plus thirty-three days after the birth of a boy, but for fourteen plus sixty-six days after the birth of a girl? Why does Christianity set an impossible standard for women in the shape of the Virgin Mary – a virgin, thus sex-denying, but a mother as well? How can any women emulate the impossible? Why does Islam demand the hiding of women's faces behind the veil, so that they will not tempt other men, a view held by orthodox Judaism as well, where married women have to cover their heads with a scarf or a wig to prevent anyone but their husbands seeing their crowning glory?

This does not look acceptable to any feminist. A feminist would ask why the liturgy is so very male, and why God is always thought of as male, a problem particularly for Christians with the Trinity. A feminist would ask why the female element of God is not more expressed, why in Judaism the role of the Shechinah, the female presence of God, is almost denied except amongst the chassidic ultra-orthodox sects. A feminist would ask why Christianity demands the impossible in virginity and motherhood, and why it is that Christianity is so negative about sex anyway. A feminist would ask why all the concern about forbidden sexual unions in Leviticus chapter eighteen and elsewhere is about penetration, and why lesbianism does not feature – and would suggest that penetration is a very male view of the sexual act. A feminist would ask why Judaism and Islam have so few female figures as role models for our daughters. At least Christianity has a fair number of female saints. A feminist would ask why wife-beating has never been taken seriously by religious organizations. And so on and so on.

For what the feminist critique of religion has done is to point out what is in fact obvious. It is not religion itself, the faith, the hope, the spirituality, the attempt to carry out God's will, which discriminates so against women. How can it, when it is all about human aspiration? It is the religious structures, carved out and forced into shape by men, which are so hostile to women, and which allow men the lions' share of public roles in religious institutions, without in any way noticing, or caring, that women are excluded. Religion itself bears no part of the blame. Faith, community, spirituality, a search for God's law, a desire to know God, wherever She might be – none of these damage women, or men. But the institutions, the laws of religious communities, the interpretation of texts, the string of texts from a male standpoint, the marginalization of women and their concerns, the failure to listen to women's voices – all these are to be laid at the feet of men, particularly men in one religious hierarchy or another, be they rabbis, priests or imams. Whether Chief Rabbi, Bishop, or Ayatollah, whether claiming seniority or acting as the humble congregational imam or rabbi or priest; it is the men who function as religious leaders who have to examine the structures of the organizations in which they find themselves, and ask themselves the hard question as honestly as they possibly can, about how they would view all this if they were female.

Some have done so. Some men, religious leaders, have campaigned long and hard for women's religious needs, feelings and status to be recognized. Those who have campaigned recently for the ordination of women to the priesthood in the Church of England did so out of a sense of justice, fair play, and the loss to the community of huge talent. So did the men in the Jewish community who first thought to train women to become rabbis, or even to educate girls in Judaism and to allow them a Bat Mitzvah as the boys had Bar Mitzvah. But there is still a huge feeling against women, in most of the mainstream religious organizations.

But, despite that, women's religious sense does not diminish. Women have found and will find, ways of expressing their spirituality and religiosity. With the advent of feminism, women are more content to be in women's groups, and some will express their religious longings alone with women. Others will seek acceptance and opportunity, increasingly available. But what remains ever clear is that women will not have true religious equality with men until they are caught up in the shaping of religious communities, and until religious communities begin to accept that much of their law and tradition is in no sense divine, but essentially human, written by men, for men, and even deliberately to keep women in their place. Women, religious as well as secular, have no intention of staying in that male-defined place. Feminism has done religious organizations nothing but good.

– 11 –

GOD AND EVIL

Karen Armstrong spent seven years as a Roman Catholic nun, has studied English literature at Oxford University, and been a teacher. Since 1982, she has been a freelance writer and broadcaster.
Her published works include *Through the Narrow Gate*, *The Gospel According to Woman*, *Muhammad*, *A History of Jerusalem*, and the best-selling *A History of God*, which has been translated into thirty langauges. Her most recent book is *In the Beginning: A New Reading of the Book of Genesis*. She teaches part-time at the Leo Baeck College for the Study of Judaism and the Training of Rabbis and Teachers.

Karen Armstrong

Human beings, be they religious or secular, cannot escape the problem of evil. We have always been simultaneously repelled and enchanted by the world about us: its beauty fills us with awe and wonder but at the same time we are appalled by the perilous nature of life on a planet where natural disasters wipe out the innocent and guilty alike, where mortality is king, to say nothing of the injustice and cruelty that we human beings inflict upon one another. Because we are meaning-seeking creatures, as soon as we fell out of the trees and became recognizably human, men and women began to create religions for themselves at the same time as they began to create works of art. Indeed, the two ventures remain deeply related: both have enabled us to cultivate a conviction that life has some ultimate meaning and value, despite the evil that surrounds us. We may not be able to define this meaning adequately but it gives us hope that all will ultimately be well, even if we find it difficult to explain our conviction in rational terms.

We are creatures who fall very easily into despair and so we need to embark on this quest for faith. Many religions begin with the perception that something has gone radically wrong with the world. The first of the Buddha's noble truths was 'Existence is suffering' (*dukkha*), though a better translation might be: 'Existence is awry'. Christians use the image of a primal fall of humanity from grace to express a similar idea. But the religions do not stop there but go on to offer a solution. Jews, Christians and Muslims have espoused monotheism, belief in a single god, whom they have portrayed in personal terms. God is all-powerful and wholly benevolent, responsible for everything that happens in the world. God is the source of all that is and will dispose all things to good. If we feel overwhelmed by the problems of evil, we must recall with Julian of Norwich that 'All shall be well.' Yet this conventional theism can result in a facile resignation. In fact monotheism demands a struggle, since it is fearfully difficult to incarnate a divine imperative in the flawed and tragic conditions of life on earth. Christians should be reminded of this every time they look at a crucifix. Muslims express it in the ideal of *jihad*, which does not simply mean 'holy war' as Western people tend to imagine, but the 'struggle' essential if men and women are to ensure that God's will prevails over evil. Over the centuries, Jews have stressed again and again that God needs human beings to act for him in this battle against the forces of darkness.

One of the greatest struggles that all monotheists have encountered is the difficulty of squaring their belief in one benevolent God with the manifest existence of evil. If God is wholly good and the creator of all things, where does evil come from? How can a deity who is omnipotent and benevolent have permitted such atrocities as the Nazi Holocaust? If God is all powerful, he could have prevented it; if for some reason, God was unable to prevent it, he is not omnipotent and cannot be the final answer to the obscenity of evil. If God could have stopped the Holocaust but chose not to, he is not only lacking in benevolence but he can be seen to be a monster.

Many have concluded as a result of such reasoning that the God of classical theism died in Auschwitz and some have preferred the secular ideal as a more honest confrontation with the problem of evil. In the secularist perspective, there is more integrity in acknowledging that there is no final solution than in the consoling illusions of religion.

It has to be said that monotheists have often made the idea of God a consoling panacea. If we consider the horrors of Auschwitz or Bosnia, the old explanation that evil is God's punishment for wrongdoing will not stand up. What kind of sin can merit suffering on such a scale? To claim that the victims will be happy hereafter in heaven – another traditional solution – is similarly facile and insulting. It can encourage religious people to abdicate from the struggle that should characterize monotheistic faith. All too often, religion has been used as an opiate that enables the devout to sing that all things are bright and beautiful, while the rich man sits in his palace, ignoring the poor man at his gate. There is also a danger that if we say that there is no evil in God we may be unable to acknowledge the evil that lurks in our own hearts, with the result that we project this evil outside ourselves and make it inhuman. In the past, Christians have cowered before Satan as just such a monstrous projection, fashioned as their own shadow-self, or they have projected this evil onto Jews or Muslims, whom they have perceived as enemies of the faith. The crusades in the Middle Ages were largely fuelled by this type of terror and denial and are an important reminder that religion has contributed in large measure to the evil in the world.

It is not surprising, therefore, that secularists have turned their backs on religion. Yet secularism has problems too. The secular ideal was born of the Enlightenment conviction that humanity could now liberate itself from the shackles of superstition and advance towards a higher state, guided by reason instead of God. But it has also been said that the hopes of the Enlightenment died in Auschwitz, since the Holocaust proved that an atheistic crusade could be just as murderous as a religious one. In recent years we have witnessed the failure of Marxism, which is an ideology that has used many aspects of the Judaeo-Christian tradition (such as its messianism and its concern for the poor and oppressed) but has eliminated all reference to transcendence or God. Marxism is, therefore, exclusively concerned with this world: there is no God, nothing that goes beyond mundane reality and it is only within the historical process that humanity will attain its final Utopian fulfilment. There is no meaning, value or reality other than its meaning in history. Consequently there can be literally no reason for not killing or enslaving other human beings if this will advance the historical process, the supreme reality. In contrast to this, the monotheistic religions have insisted that every event in this world has a transcendent dimension, a dimension symbolized in such ideas as 'God' or the Last Judgement. Jews, Christians and Muslims have all in their different ways seen God in the workings of history and, at its best, their religion has taught them that the eternal fate of an individual is more important than the course of history.

A principled, passionate secularism (such as that expressed in the ideal of liberal humanism) will vehemently reject the excesses of Marxism but it will also eschew the idea of the transcendent. A secularist will claim that we can be good without a divine overseer, who, it has to be admitted, has been represented all too often as a sort of cosmic Big Brother. Secularism is a noble ideal, because it wants to redeem humanity from the excesses of religion, some of which we have considered above. Religion is not necessarily about God: Buddhists, for example, often view the monotheistic conception of the divine as so limited as to be almost blasphemous. In the same way, perhaps, we can see a secular humanism as a religion without God that has its own disciplines of mind and heart. A humanist will be deeply committed to the inalienable and inviolable (I had almost said 'sacred') dignity of human life and will struggle, like the true monotheist, to assert the paramount importance of the individual. But can secularism dispense with the transcendent altogether, particularly that transcendence which religious people encounter in the ground of their own being and within other people?

All the great world religions have agreed that human life contains an element that transcends or goes beyond it. They referred to this by different names. Buddhists call it Nirvana, Hindus call it Brahman and monotheists call it God. Further, in their different ways, they have insisted that this mysterious reality is not just something encountered outside the self but that it is inextricably involved with humanity. The transcendent element is not alien to human beings – this is why Buddhists reject the notion of the supernatural – but is an essential aspect of our being. It is a reality at one and the same time transcendent and immanent, subjective and objective. We could not prove its existence rationally, simply because the transcendent of its very nature must go beyond all our words and concepts. But it was nevertheless experienced as a fact of life by people of all conditions and in all cultures in the pre-modern world. Our modern scientific society has tended to edit out this sense of the sacred and people tend to approach even religious truth in a literal rather than in a symbolic mode. Nevertheless, even the most thoroughgoing secularists have experienced transcendence while listening to a great piece of music or when reading a poem that touches something deeply buried within and lifts them momentarily beyond themselves. Just for a few seconds, at such times, we have the conviction that all is well and has ultimate meaning, even though we would be hard put to explain or prove this momentary perception. So, whether it is experienced within or outside of religion, this transcendence is natural to the human condition and, however we choose to interpret it, has been a fact of human life.

The religions have tried to help men and women to transform this experience of transcendence or 'God' into a moral ethic. All the great world religions insist that the only authentic test of a religious experience is that it issues in practical compassion for our fellow human beings. Often this imperative has been interpreted inadequately: we have been taught that God will punish us or that we will go to Hell if we treat others badly. But this bowdlerizes the essential religious conviction that all human beings must be revered because they are, quite literally, sacred. The transcendence that gives life its ultimate meaning, that exists ineffably beyond us (Nirvana, God, Brahman) also inheres within each one of us. Hindus join their hands and bow to one another in greeting to acknowledge that they are encountering the divinity in their neighbour.

Shakespeare expresses this insight in a secularist mode in *Hamlet*, a play that celebrates the new humanism that was emerging in Europe. Hamlet may have studied in Wittenburg, Luther's city, but in many respects he belongs more to the Renaissance than the Reformation:

> What a piece of work is a man! how noble in reason! how infinite in faculty! In form, in moving, how express and admirable! in action, how like an angel! In appearance, how like a god! The beauty of the world!

It is Hamlet's tragedy that he is so surrounded by evil that he can no longer be delighted by humanity, which appears to him a mere 'quintessence of dust'. There is murder, betrayal and cruelty in Elsinore, including the evil within Hamlet himself. People simply manipulate others to suit their own ends. In a key scene, Hamlet asks the sycophantic but treacherous Guildenstern to play a recorder for him. When Guildenstern repeatedly protests that he has no musical skill and cannot command the pipe 'to any utterance of harmony', Hamlet bursts out:

> Why, look you now, how unworthy a thing you make of me!
> You would play upon me; you would seem to know my stops;
> you would pluck out the heart of my mystery.

The fact that each one of us remains a mystery, even to ourselves, transcending all the perceptions and insights of others, however wise, is an insight that lies at the heart of both liberal humanism and religion at their best. If carefully cultivated, this perception will help us to acquire that absolute respect for one another that is due to the mystery that monotheists call 'God'. When we encounter another human being, the sacred mystery that he or she incarnates should challenge us, give us the same kind of salutary shock as a strictly divine theophany. If we recognize that sacred mystery at the heart of the other we will not be able to exploit, kill, enslave or torture any human being for our own purposes since this would be blasphemy.

As far as we know, dogs have no difficulty living up to their canine nature but men and women seem to find it very hard to live up to their humanity. Consequently each of the great religions have insisted that we learn on a daily basis to recognize the mystery within ourselves and one another. Jesus was not the only Jew to declare that the commandment: 'Thou shalt love thy neighbour as thyself' was the great principle of the Law of Moses, equal to the command to love God himself. In the Talmud, the rabbis taught that offences against a fellow human being were a denial of God, tantamount to atheism, and that to humiliate even a slave was equivalent to murder, itself a sacrilegious denial of God's existence. It is in this spirit that Christians are taught to see Christ in their neighbours, especially in the needy, the disgraced and the marginalized. In the Koran, God is experienced as an imperative to succour the poor and the oppressed: the great symbol (*aya*) of the Last Judgement insists over and over again that the eternal fate of the individual is the paramount religious concern.

It was this conviction that humanity and divinity are inseparable and that neither can be seen in isolation from the other that informs the Christian doctrine of incarnation or the Shiite belief in the immanence of God in certain privileged descendants of the Prophet Muhammad and his ward, Ali. The whole monotheistic insistence that the mysterious transcendence that we call 'God' should be conceived as personal has helped Jews, Christians and Muslims to cultivate this appreciation of the sacredness of personality. But notions of God and transcendence, however beloved and hallowed by tradition, can only be provisional. Monotheists have always insisted that it is idolatrous to confuse human images of the divine with the indescribable mystery itself. Some of the notions of God as a personality like ourselves writ large with likes and dislikes similar to our own have inspired abhorrent behaviour and many people today find them incredible. But for 4000 years, people have been changing their conception of God, often in surprising and dramatic ways. There is no reason why we, in the late twentieth century, should not change our perception of the divine to meet the particular needs and tragedy of our time.

Some people have suggested that we should replace our image of God as omnipotent for a suffering, impotent God. This is a perception that has figured importantly in both the Jewish and the Christian traditions in the past. The startling idea that the *Shekinah*, the divine presence, had actually gone into exile with the Jews after the destruction of their temple by the Romans in 70 CE gave them the courage to endure the trauma of their own exile. Even more audacious notions of the divine exile were devised by the Kabbalist Isaac Luria in the sixteenth century after the Jews had been expelled from Spain. Another way that we might try to think about God and the encounter with evil is based on the older creation myths that we find in the Bible. In the first chapter of Genesis, the priestly author showed God calmly bringing order out of chaos, separating light from darkness, night from day, dry land from sea. This God is in complete control of the cosmos: no effort is involved in keeping the destructive forces within bounds. But this image of God, developed in the sixth century BCE, was an innovation. The Bible also preserves older creation stories that were more in line with the pagan mythology of the Near East. These show the god YHWH engaged in mortal combat with the monsters of chaos; his victory is not taken for granted. In these old tales, the creator-god is often almost destroyed and the destructive forces of evil never wholly overcome. The struggle against evil is one in which God and humanity are ceaselessly engaged. Each year the god's victory was celebrated in the temples of the Near East, including the Temple in Jerusalem; the ritual celebrated the eternal struggle that people could discern at the core of existence and enabled them to commit themselves to the ongoing battle for goodness, order and peace. Perhaps we could think about God in these terms today as we recoil from the suffering and evil that seems to erupt in all parts of the globe.

The trouble is that in many religious circles the very idea that the God of classical theism no longer serves our needs is regarded as blasphemous. But perhaps religious people should recall that monotheism has always been concerned about the sin of idolatry. Idolatry does not simply mean bowing down to worship a statue. It also means giving absolute sanction to any human image of the divine. If we think that classical theism is the last word on God, we are in danger of being idolaters because, as the greatest monotheists in all three traditions have long insisted, all our ideas about the divine are inadequate and provisional and cannot measure up to the ineffable Reality itself. Theology is only a *façon de parler*. Today more and more people are becoming disenchanted with the conventional forms of religion in Britain. There is a hunger for spirituality but all too often the hungry sheep look up and are not fed. Has there been any real effort to grapple creatively with the problem of evil as it has been revealed to us in this century? Both Christians and Jews have some hard thinking to do about the Holocaust, for example, from two very different perspectives. The evil that appeared in Auschwitz should perhaps nudge us out of a weary, inadequate theism. It is not sufficient to try to juggle with our old theological ideas. We need to use the horrors of Auschwitz, Bosnia and Rwanda to appreciate anew the absolute mystery of God. In the Hindu world, evil can be one of the masks of the divine: we should not imagine that, as religious people we have all the answers. When we face the darkness that lies at the heart of the human personality, we must realize that we have come to the end of what ordinary ideologies and explanations can do and are up against life's ultimate mystery.

All the religions of the world insist that the prime duty is compassion. Our rabbis, priests, ministers and imams need to help us to cultivate that absolute respect for the sacred identity of others in order to shield them from the voraciousness of our own egotism. This should be the top priority. But all too often, churches, synagogues and mosques retreat from this duty.

Instead there is endless and acrimonious argument about whether women can be rabbis or priests; whether a particular theology is compatible with the tradition; whether contraception is permissible; whether Salman Rushdie deserves the death penalty. As long as religious people waste their creative energies in this way and neglect the 'one thing necessary' they will have failed the test of the late twentieth century. Secularists sometimes point out that religious people are more often behind war than peace at the present time: in Northern Ireland, Bosnia and the Middle East, it is often the case that secularists are more committed to peace than their religious fellow countrymen. Secularists are right to look askance at such belligerence: it is a scandal and one of the ways in which religion has failed in our time.

In this tragic world, it is not easy to have faith that life has ultimate value nor to curb the evil impulse within ourselves. It is all too easy for us to become paralysed, like Hamlet, who was not rescued from his despair by either the Protestant ideal of salvation nor the more secular ideology of the Renaissance. Religious people can so easily waste time on inessentials that they should recall that their prime concern, one shared by the secularist, is to cultivate a sense of life's irreducible mystery, especially as this is revealed to us in other suffering human beings.

– 12 –

THE MORAL CASE AGAINST GOD

Richard Harries is the author of eighteen books, including *Art and the Beauty of God* (Mowbray) which was selected as a book of the year by Anthony Burgess in *The Observer*. His most recent book *Questioning Belief* (SPCK) explores fundamental questions of faith and doubt. In 1996 he was elected a fellow of the Royal Society of Literature.
Dr Harries has been Bishop of Oxford since 1987. Before that he was Dean of King's College London. He is Chairman of the Council of Christians and Jews, Chairman of the Church of England's Board of Social Responsibility and active in the House of Lords on Social and Moral Issues.

RICHARD HARRIES
BISHOP OF OXFORD

MOST PEOPLE who think seriously about religion focus on the philosophical difficulties of belief. How do we know there is a God? Indeed, what do we mean by the very word? It is this that has given rise to the long, sophisticated tradition of argumentation over the various proofs for the existence of God.

I believe that today such arguments are a distraction from the real issues. They divert attention from where, in fact, most people's worries about religion lie, though they may rarely dare to voice their concern. This seldom articulated feeling is that the case for religion is morally unacceptable. It is to be rejected not primarily on philosophical grounds but on ethical ones, as morally flawed, even evil. Here I am using the Christian faith as a paradigm, for it is the only religion I know from the inside. As for other religions, I can only say, 'Where the cap fits … '

My own view is that religious belief is entirely natural and it is both right and inevitable that it should be so – whether or not the claims made by a particular religion are true or not. A child brought up in a loving and stable home will quite naturally want to think that there is a wise and loving power behind life itself. Making instinctive use of the argument from causality, the child will be led to think that the universe must have a creator; and knowing goodness in their own family life will quite understandably want to assume that this creator is good. If a child is taught to pray, even minimally, at home or school, then this natural movement of the mind will be reinforced. So it is that in every culture and in every period of history, religion has played a central role, even though the form of that religion has of course varied. Thinking oneself out of the dominant religion of one's own culture has, until the enlightenment, been a singular thing to do.

I stress the point that religious belief is natural, in the sense that I have described, not to argue that it is thereby true but in order better to sharpen the focus of what the real quarrel is about. This includes the ancient dilemma of evil and suffering, of how the presence of so much anguish in the world can be reconciled with belief in a loving creator, but it goes beyond this. This essay is not concerned with the problem of suffering as such, though that is where it starts. For it was Ivan Karamazov in Dostoevsky's great novel who began the modern protest against God on moral grounds. Hearing stories about cruelty to children, Ivan argues that no heaven could make good what has occurred; nothing can justify a creation in which such things happen:

> If the sufferings of children go to make up the sum of sufferings which is necessary for the purchase of truth, then I say beforehand that the entire truth is not worth such a price. We cannot afford to pay so much for admission … It is not God that I do not accept Alyosha merely that I most respectfully return him the ticket.[1]

---

1 Dostoevsky, F.M., *The Brothers Karamazov* (Penguin, 1976) vol. 1, p. 287.

For Ivan Karamazov, God may very well exist. but a God who allows such a creation as ours cannot be accepted. The ticket is most respectfully returned. What was happening in Dostoevsky's mind was also occurring in England in a less dramatic way. Surveying the rise of agnosticism in the 19th century, Alec Vidler wrote that it was not due to the rise of science or biblical criticism but because what Christianity called upon people to believe with such a sense of its own superiority struck them as morally inferior to their own highest beliefs and standards. The protest was there too in the 18th century, paradoxically emerging with particular clarity in one of the most devout, troubled, souls of the age, Dr Johnson. His rejection of a particular understanding of God is fired with a sense of bitter outrage. In his review of a book by Soame Jenyns, Johnson writes:

> That a set of beings unseen and unheard are hovering about us, trying experiments upon our sensibility, putting us in agonies to see our limbs quiver, torturing us to madness that they may laugh at our vagaries, sometimes obstructing the bile that they may see how a man looks when he is yellow; sometimes breaking a traveller's bones to try how he will get home; sometimes wasting a man to a skeleton, and sometimes killing him fat for the greater elegance of his hide? This is an account of natural evil which though, like the rest, not quite new, is very entertaining though I know not how much it may contribute to patience.[2]

The reason why so few people have voiced this strain of disbelief is no mystery. Until recently God and the good were equated in the minds of most people. Religion was, by definition, a good thing, the source and standard of all goodness. So people could hardly even begin to think themselves into the position of criticizing religion on moral grounds. Moreover such criticism would have posed an enormous emotional, psychological, social and political threat. It is only now, with a growing disassociation of religion and morality, that the underlying moral criticism of religion can come to the fore. This moral protest is more often than not simply a confused, inarticulate sense that an aspect of received religion is inimical to the human spirit, or anti-human in some way and because such feelings have been regarded as unacceptable as they still are for most believers today, they have not been taken out and examined as systematically as they might be. Apart from the major question of how we can reconcile the presence of so much evil and suffering in the world with a belief that it owes its origins to a good God, several elements can be identified.

First, there is the picture of God, particularly in the Old Testament, sending diseases, destroying cities, killing people through natural disaster and urging one group of human beings to kill another through war. Believers tend simply to live with such a picture on the assumption that it is a view of God that belongs to the early stage of human religious understanding, one that we have long since outgrown. But it still comes as a shock to those who look at the Bible for the first time or who

---

2 Johnson, Samuel, 'Review of Soame Jenyns', *The Oxford Authors* (OUP, 1984) p. 535.

come to it afresh. Brian Keenan, when a hostage in the Lebanon, experienced the reality of God in an overwhelming way and began to read the Bible. Both he and John McCarthy found great solace in reading the Psalms. However, as Keenan wrote: 'The blood and gore of the Old Testament stories horrified me.'[3] That is a mild reaction compared with that of the late Randolph Churchill. Whilst serving in Yugoslavia during the Second World War his companions, including Evelyn Waugh, got so fed up with his continual talking that they took him on a bet that he could not read the whole Bible through from beginning to end. They hoped in this way to shut him up for a bit but they were disappointed. After every few verses Randolph Churchill would explode: 'God, isn't God a shit.' When I quoted that story a few years ago in a devotional article for a church newspaper, the expletive was expurgated. That was understandable. Nevertheless, Randolph Churchill's blunt, foul-mouthed utterance puts into words what some devout people feel but dare not say.

The second area of moral protest concerns particular doctrines, most obviously the idea that God sentences people to eternal punishment in hell. F.D. Maurice lost his job at King's College, London in the 19th century for casting doubt on this view. If we have been created free, then we can always create our own hell even in the midst of heaven, but the idea of God banishing people eternally from his presence seems difficult to reconcile with any ordinary concept of loving kindness.

Another view that has morally objectionable aspects is the so-called penal substitutionary theory of the Atonement. All Christians are agreed that Christ, through his life, death and resurrection, and the continuing presence of the Holy Spirit, makes us one with God. However, the Church has never had any official view about how this is so. In the New Testament, there are a range of metaphors which try to explore this mystery and one of them certainly suggests that through the Incarnation God enters into the darkness consequent upon human sinfulness. But this is very different from the view which sees it as a legal transaction. According to that theory, as human beings we all deserve eternal punishment. However, on the Cross, Jesus suffered this eternal punishment instead of us. If we accept this fact and put our trust in him, we will no longer go to hell but will live with God for ever. It is a picture that is a million miles away from the understanding of God Jesus put before us, both in his own life and in such stories as the Parable of the Prodigal Son.

The third objection focuses on the authoritarian, law-based aspect of religion which, so it is held, can only encourage infantilism. Maturity, on any ordinary definition, involves standing on our own two feet and taking responsibility for our lives. We wrestle with the decisions we have to make, taking help from where we

---

3 Keenan, Brian, *An Evil Cradling* (Vintage, 1992) p. 187.

can, including the wisdom accumulated in laws and rules. However, in the end we have to make up our own mind. A religion that stresses only obedience to God, who lays down laws that have to be obeyed willy-nilly, seems designed to keep human beings in a state of permanent dependence and immaturity. Mr. Polly in one of H.G. Wells's novels considered God to be:

> a limitless being having the nature of a school master and making infinite rules, known and unknown, rules that were always ruthlessly enforced and with an infinite capacity for punishment, and most horrible of all to think of, limitless powers of espial.[4]

Such a God, a regimental sergeant-major writ large in the skies, is a caricature of Christian understanding. Nevertheless, it is one that sometimes comes across and insofar as it does, people find it morally intolerable.

The fourth objection focuses on the orientation of religion to a life beyond this one. Instead of that, we should be striving to improve conditions here on earth. I believe that the driving force behind both the Marxist and the Freudian criticism of religion was a moral one. In the name of a perfect human society of the future Marx criticized religion as a misplaced hope, leading to resignation rather than struggle. In order that humans might become properly and fully human in a better society, religion had to be put aside. Indeed he believed that the criticism of religion was the beginning of all criticism.

In a similar way although Freud was concerned with the psychological processes that bring about religious belief, he was concerned to help people face up to the reality of the present world. It is no accident that both Karl Marx and Sigmund Freud had a Jewish background. The moral values and passion in their work was imbibed from their Jewish upbringing and fed their attacks on religion, in the name of a better humanity and a better society in the future. They believed that religion did actual harm, in stopping people facing up to the reality of the present and struggling to do something about it. Religion inculcated attitudes of obedience, resignation, passivity and dependence. From a philosophical standpoint, Nietzsche can also be included in this category, with his fierce attacks on Christianity as bringing about what he regarded as such weak qualities as opposed to the strong ones necessary for humanity in the future.

I would also place feminist criticisms of traditional Christianity at this point. From a feminist perspective received religion is not only hierarchical and authoritarian but patriarchal. To the criticisms of Marx, Freud and Nietzsche is added the further one, that it reinforces male dominance; that the people who are meant to be obedient, resigned and passive are women. This in turn raises questions about the God who apparently sanctions such a system. As Celie says in Alice Walker's novel *The Colour Purple*:

---

4   Quoted by Williams, H.A., 'Psychological Objections' in *Objections to Christian Belief* (Constable, 1963) p. 50.

> Man corrupt everything … He tried to make you think he everywhere. Soon as you think he everywhere, you think he God, but he aint. Whenever you trying to pray, and man plop himself on the other end of it, tell him to git lost.[5]

Then, finally, there is a close connection between a number of the foregoing criticisms and the sense that religion is of its nature anti-human and anti-life. Either it provides a set of stereotyped attitudes and responses which blunts the sensitivity to things as they are or it oppresses us and blocks our love for life. The result is that human truth, especially that conveyed by artistic forms of various kinds, has sometimes been asserted by those in rebellion against the religion of their childhood. Stephen Dedalus in James Joyce's novel *Portrait of an Artist as a Young Man* stands for very many. Stephen was seriously debating in his mind whether he should become a priest but one day, as he walked on the beach, life, as he put it, took hold of him. He described his mood in these words.

> His throat ached with a desire to cry aloud, the cry of a hawk or eagle on high, to cry piercingly of his deliverance to the winds … This was the call of life to his soul not the dull gross voice of the world of duties and despair, not the inhuman voice that had called him to the pale service of the altar. His soul had arisen from the grave of boyhood, spurning her grave clothes … The clouds were drifting above him silently and silently the sea tangle was drifting below him and the grey warm air was still and a new wild life was singing in his veins.[6]

He decides to leave Ireland altogether and the night before he goes he wrote in his diary: 'Welcome, O life! I go to encounter for the millionth time the reality of experience.'

Wilfred Owen too thought of becoming an Anglican priest. In a poem entitled 'Maundy Thursday' but which should in fact be called Good Friday because it describes the service of the Veneration of the Cross which happens on that day, Owen depicts himself coming to kneel and kiss the Cross.

> Then I, too, knelt before that acolyte.
> Above the Crucifix I bent my head:
> The Christ was thin, and cold and very dead:
> And yet I bowed, yea, kissed – my lips did cling.
> (I kissed the warm live hand that held the thing).[7]

Religion, he felt, belonged to the dead past. What he responded to was living humanity.

So the moral case against religion is a formidable one, even without taking into account the fundamental question of how we are to reconcile the existence of so much suffering in the world with its creation by a loving God.

---

5 Walker, Alice, *The Colour Purple* (Women's Press, 1983).

6 Joyce, James, *Portrait of an Artist as a Young Man*.

7 Owen, Wilfred, 'Maundy Thursday', *War Poems and Others*, ed. Dominic Hibberd (Chatto and Windus, 1973) p. 55.

I would not remain a believer if I did not think that something could be said in relation to all the objections so far raised. But I do not want in any way to underestimate the force of those objections or the passion with which they can be held. This is not the point to put forward other considerations which place the objections in a somewhat different perspective, for my purpose is to build up the picture of a particular kind of secular humanist, one who is not totally opposed to the possibility of religious truth on philosophical grounds but who finds religion morally objectionable for one or other of the reasons adduced. This is someone who seeks to stand on their own two feet, responsible for their own life and actions, sensitive to the terrible suffering in life and active, both personally and politically, in doing something about it. They do not know if life has any ultimate meaning and purpose. It seems unlikely. But this does not mean that their personal life is meaningless. On the contrary, they give meaning to their own life by living with compassion, courage and humour.

Valuing the arts as a source of inspiration, solace and even meaning, they mostly find life worthwhile. If towards the end, the prospect of life becomes unbearable through a debilitating illness, they would seriously contemplate euthanasia. Once, when they were young, they were great talkers against religion. Now they are older, they recognize there are good people with many beliefs they do not share, they live and let live and, who knows, despite everything, there might be something in it after all. But it still seems to hinder much of what they believe in, it still has its morally objectionable aspects.

For the life of such a secular humanist, I would want to offer two cheers. More than that, I would want to offer thanks for all that is healthy and worthwhile in such a life and for the manifestation of many admirable moral qualities.

I believe that something can and must be said in relation to the moral objections to religion sketched out earlier. Yet none of the arguments I could put forward will of themselves tip the balance unless I had, prior to all and undergirding all, belief in a God who seems to me supremely morally attractive. This is a God whose 'nature and name is love', to use the words of Charles Wesley's great hymn.

In Evelyn Waugh's *Decline and Fall* Mr Prendergast lost his faith and gave up being a Church of England clergyman because he could never work out why God had created the universe in the first place. He had no difficulty in believing the miracles which others find a stumbling block to belief but he never could answer the big question.

> Once granted the first step, I can see that everything else follows – Tower of Babel, Babylonian captivity, Incarnation, Church, Bishops, incense, everything – but what I couldn't see, and what I can't see now, is *why* did it all begin?[8]

8 Waugh, Evelyn, *Decline and Fall* (Penguin, 1980) p. 33.

The answer to this question can only be one that is similar to the question of why human parents continue to have children. It is the nature of love to create, to bring into existence lives that are more than simply a projection of our own. It is the nature of God, who is in his being eternal love, to create. This creation is not just tossed off in an idle moment. Into it God pours his very self. As W.H. Vanstone explored so profoundly in *Love's Endeavour, Love's Expense*, all that God is, goes into creating us.

Then, for a Christian, the same God who pours himself out into his creation, empties himself into the life of a vulnerable human being.

> Have this mind among yourselves, which you have in Christ Jesus, who, though he was in the form of God, did not count equality with God a thing to be grasped, but emptied himself, taking the form of a servant, being born in the likeness of men. And being found in human form he humbled himself and became obedient unto death, even on a Cross.
>
> (*Philippians* 2, 5–8)

The Eternal Son of God comes amongst us to break down the barriers of pride and suspicion, through his very weakness, and to bring us into a new relationship with himself.

This God is above all a God of spiritual beauty. The beauty which we discern in nature and the arts has its origin in God himself. 'The beauty of holiness' which we can sometimes glimpse in the humility and godliness of another human being, again has its origin in God himself. Both the material beauty in nature and the arts and the spiritual beauty which we can glimpse in the saints, are pointers to the divine glory – that sublime conjunction of truth, goodness and beauty which is God himself. It is this which overwhelmed Moses on Mount Sinai. It is this that shone through in Jesus on the Mount of Transfiguration.

> For it is the God who said, 'Let light shine out of darkness', who has shone in our hearts to give the light of the knowledge of the glory of God in the face of Christ.
>
> (2 *Corinthians*, 4, 6)

Rose Macauley had a wonderful sense of this 'luminous enchantment'. In her novel *The Towers of Trebizond*, she knows that because of factors in her own life she is at the moment outside the city of God. Yet she still feels its overwhelming attraction.

> Still the Towers of Trebizond, the fabled city, shimmers on a far horizon, gated and walled and held in a luminous enchantment. It seems that for me, and however much I must stand outside them this must for ever be.[9]

Having something of that sense, in however a flickering, partial way, I cannot but believe that those who do not share it are deprived. In however many other ways their lives might be rich, richer than mine, in this, the most fundamental way of all, there is a terrible loss.

---

9 Macauley, Rose, *The Towers of Trebizond* (Collins, 1956) p. 288.

For the secular humanist life has in the end no meaning or purpose other than that which he or she can bestow upon it. The values they cherish of compassion, courage and humour are pitted against the abyss. Life has a heart of darkness. It is therefore very understandable that a fair number of secular humanists, sensitive to the terrible anguish of life, its cruelty and suffering, should be prone to an inner despair. They are not clinically depressed. They keep up appearances in a wonderful way, so often the life and soul of any gathering. But alone in the quiet moments of the night they have to face the fact that it is a tale, 'a tale of sound and fury signifying nothing'. Or like Jonathan Swift or Edwin Muir, they look at their fellow human beings, without souls, stripped of any eternal aura, and see simply animals, and the experience is a devastating one.

We are endlessly resourceful in covering this up and it is a well-known fact that some of the greatest humorists and cartoonists are most acutely aware of what is at stake. Yet others, because of what is involved, steadfastly avoid thinking through the consequences of their disbelief. They treat it as a trivial matter. The late, lamented John Harriott put it well:

> As a heavy reader and radio listener I cannot count the times when writers and speakers seem to feel obliged to preface their remarks by announcing their disdain for religion. 'Of course, I'm not religious myself', 'I've no time for religion', 'I was brought up a Catholic … I had a convent education … but.' But what? 'But I've grown out of all that rubbish, I've seen through it all. Now I breathe a larger air. Now you can be sure I'm bright and sensible, sound in mind and fully qualified to be heard here.' The idea that you have to be dumb to be religious, that religion is a, thankfully, lost cause, is the new intellectual slavery. Dissidents are at best strange zoological specimens.

Religion, God knows, has much to answer for; the crimes and absurdities committed in its name are many.

> But strangest of all is the curious assumption that to close the door on religion is to step into a wider world. Argue by all means that the believer's universe is all delusion, but not that a vision of human life stretching beyond time and space is smaller than one that sees it ending in a handful of dust … And that to believe human beings are infinitely precious to God, reflecting his nature which they are born to share, and by grace can stretch their powers beyond their natural reach, is somehow less enriching and enlarging than to think them just animal slime. Delusion it may be, but at least a delusion of grandeur. Delusion it may be, but at least a dynamic delusion, adding point and energy and nobility to life. And to reject it, if rejected it must be, is hardly a matter for self-congratulation, but rather for mourning and drawing down of blinds.[10]

There is also the further question whether secular humanism can provide a strong enough foundation of morality on which society can be built. Every human civilization to date rests upon a vision of the world which is at once religious and moral.

---

10 Harriot, John, The Tablet.

Moral values, qualities and codes have been understood as springing from an essentially religious understanding of human existence. Alasdair MacIntyre's seminal work *After Virtue*, traces the history of moral philosophy and shows how moral values and virtues are always embedded in a particular historical context. The individualism and fragmentation of modern society is reflected in the disarray of moral philosophy which is characterized by endless disagreements about the most fundamental things. He ends his book on a now famous and somewhat despairing note, namely that we need a contemporary equivalent of the Benedictine movement to see us through new dark ages; we need communities of people in which there is a religious vision that undergirds and sets forth a moral one.

I am totally opposed to any idea that religion ought to be used to prop up a failing morality. The only reason for adhering to a religion is because you believe it to be true. But if you believe it to be true it immediately sets the moral quest in a new, more alluring perspective. The question remains whether, without that perspective, moral values by themselves can win the hearts and minds of the mass of human beings.

Few have felt the dilemma as acutely as the novelist and poet Stevie Smith. For much of her life a believing Anglican, she knew the power of Christian faith to captivate and enthral the heart. She also came to think that some aspects of Christian belief were morally repugnant. In her poem, 'How do you see' she writes about the Holy Spirit.

> Yes, it is a beautiful idea, one of the most
> Beautiful ideas Christianity has ever had,
> This idea of the Spirit of God, the Holy Ghost,
> My heart goes out to this beautiful Holy Ghost,
> He is so beautifully inhuman, he is like the fresh air.

Yet, she feels, we have to put away such ideas.

> Oh I know we must put away the beautiful fairy stories
> And learn to be good in a dull way without enchantment,
> Yes, we must.

Then she ends:

> Oh how sad it is to give up the Holy Ghost
> He is so beautiful, but not when you look close,
> And the consolations of religion are so beautiful,
> But not when you look close. ...
>
> Oh Christianity, Christianity,
> That has grown kinder now, as in the political world
> The colonial system grows kinder before it vanishes,
> Are you vanishing?
> Is it not time for you to vanish?

> I do not think we shall be able to bear much longer the dishonesty
> Of clinging for comfort to beliefs we do not believe in,
> For comfort, and to be comfortably free of the fear
> Of diminishing good, as if truth were a convenience.
> I think if we do not learn quickly, and learn to teach children,
> To be good without enchantment, without the help
> Of beautiful painted fairy stories pretending to be true,
> Then I think it will be too much for us, the dishonesty,
> And, armed as we are now, we shall kill everybody,
> It will be too much for us, we shall kill everybody.[11]

The anguish in that poem needs little comment. It presses a question to which no secular humanist can confidentially give the answer yes.

If all religious claims are untrue, then it is better to face the fact that life is, from this point of view, bleak, that there is no ultimate meaning or purpose to it and that we have to construct a morality as best we can knowing it goes against the grain of the universe. But we should not pretend that there is anything less than the most terrible loss if there is no 'luminous enchantment.' And we cannot be at all confident that we can 'learn to be good in a dull way without enchantment.'

So my two cheers for secular humanism are expressions of gratitude for moral values asserted with a kind of defiance, against an underlying metaphysical despair. The fact that there cannot be a third cheer can only be cause for sadness. Yet even in that metaphysical despair, I can discern a contradiction and therefore a hope, even if it is not one acknowledged by the person themselves.

This is perhaps seen most clearly in those who now look to the arts as a justification of existence. Anthony Storr's book *Music and the Mind* ends on this theme, a position he himself seems to take. It was also explicit in Nietzsche. Nietzsche wrote:

> The metaphysical comfort – with which, I am suggesting even now, every true tragedy leaves us – that life is at the bottom of things, despite all the changes of appearances, indestructibly powerful and pleasurable. Tragedy does *not* teach resignation – To represent terrible and questionable things is in itself an instinct for power and magnificence in an artist: he does not fear them – there is no such thing as pessimistic art – art affirms … For a philosopher to say, 'The good and the beautiful are one', is infamy: if he goes on to add, 'Also the true', one ought to thrash him. Truth is ugly. we possess *art* lest we *perish of the truth*.[12]

There is however a fundamental contradiction or paradox here. Nietzsche is maintaining that truth is ugly and that art must represent the dark side of things, as indeed it must. He then goes on to say that in doing this art affirms. It reveals life to be, despite everything, pleasurable. Even tragedy brings metaphysical comfort. But

11 Smith, Stevie, 'How do you see?' *The Collected Poems of Stevie Smith*, (Penguin 20th Century Classics, 1975) p. 516–21. Courtesy of James McGibbon.

12 Storr, Anthony, *Music and the Mind*.

this is to affirm, through art, that not all truth is ugly, that there is a beautiful face to life as well as a terrible one. In short, truth is shown holding hands with the beautiful (art) and the good (the moral vision which is expressed in the art). Nietzsche says that, 'We posses art lest we perish of the truth.' But, in possessing art, we reveal that the truth does not simply destroy: it comforts and affirms.

Anthony Storr, summing up Nietzsche but I suspect also putting forward his own view, says that in listening to certain kinds of music, 'We have moved beyond mere enjoyment of music to a condition in which we are saying, "Yes" to life as it actually is: tragic, ecstatic, painful, and joyful.'

I believe that this is indeed the experience of great art, particularly art that focuses on the tragic side of life; but this means that truth is *not* totally ugly. Truth is *not* such as we only perish from it. We say 'Yes' to life because there is that in life which draws forth that 'Yes'. That 'Yes' is not an arbitrary choice, it is a response to something in life, as captured by art, which is actually there. For a Christian, as for many others, what is there has its origin in the Creation story itself, when it is remarked: 'And God saw everything that he had made, and behold, it was very good.' And it is very good because it springs from the hands of a good Creator.

– 13 –

LIVING WITHOUT GOD

John Mortimer is internationally acclaimed as a playwright and author, but he is also a QC and supporter of many causes. His current responsibilities include being Chairman of the Royal Society of Literature and of the Royal Court Theatre and President of the Howard League for Penal Reform.
Through television and books Rumpole has become one of our best loved national characters but he represents only a small part of John Mortimer's output for television, film and books. The second part of his autobiography *Murder and other Friends* was published in 1994.

JOHN MORTIMER

WHEN we start discussing our beliefs we have to acknowledge that we have only a little more free choice in such matters than we have in our height, the colour of our skin or the shape of our noses. Very few Eskimos become Hindus, few of those brought up in Outer Mongolia become Wesleyan Methodists. The children of devout Catholics or Muhammadans follow in their parents' pilgrimages. Our childhood, our upbringing and place of birth determine our beliefs, and few people, having reached an age of independence, make a careful study of the world's varieties of faith and reach a calm and independent choice. What we believe depends, to a large extent, on who and what we are.

So I should start by connecting my beliefs with my origins. My father was a convinced Darwinian who told me that seven days' labour would not have produced a horse, which evolved over the centuries, let alone *homo sapiens*. My mother was a Shavian New Woman. Their politics were liberal, I'm sure they believed in progress, assisted by the process of evolution. Neither of them believed in a personal God. However, their standards of morality were high, my mother looked after my irascible father, read his briefs to him and cut up his food at meal times in a way which many people found to be saintly. My father, although he made a joke of most things, was serious about professional ethics and decent behaviour, and if I am forced to make a moral, or indeed a literary decision, I am content to refer it to his memory. I am also proud of the fact that neither my father's blindness nor his approaching death caused him to turn to God. He was able to deal with such matters by a stoicism, more common in his generation, and by his own particular view of the universe.

So I came from a home without religious belief, and when I got to my prep school in the early 1930s, only a dozen or so years after the Great War, the Christianity I met was involved with ideas of patriotism, Empire and military duty. Indeed, the clergymen who preached to us spoke with nostalgia of straffing 'jerry' in the last war, and seemed to be looking forward to doing the same thing to him in the next. I remember joining in a hymn at school, singing: 'Only believe and you shall see That Christ is all in all to thee.' I think I did my best. I tried to believe, but the vision eluded me. Religious faith, the power to make a leap in the dark and believe in what appears to be irrational, is a talent I was born without. I have never been able, even in that period of trying, to accept the idea of an all powerful, all wise and loving God who presides over our destinies and will end by judging us according to what have always seemed to me his peculiar, and not easily defensible, standards.

If God existed I'm not sure I'd like him very much. This is a dangerous statement for an unbeliever because it's hard to dislike something, or someone, that doesn't exist. But let us suppose there is an all loving and omnipotent deity and ask him why he sat back and permitted the Holocaust, the massacres and ethnic cleansing in Yugoslavia and the mass murders in Stalin's Russia, to take only three charges in the long and blood-stained indictment of human history. When he heard that his wife and children had been butchered by Macbeth's thugs, MacDuff called out to God: 'Did heaven look on, and would not take their part?' The question has never been answered to MacDuff's satisfaction – or indeed to mine.

The standard explanation is that we were given free will which enables us to choose between good and evil. This may be very satisfactory for the concentration camp guards and assassins who can choose whether or not to commit their crimes; but the innocent men, women and children whom they march into the gas ovens, or whose throats they slit, have no free will to exercise in the matter. Children who die of leukaemia, or perish in floods and earthquakes, are also unable to exercise 'free will'.

I have asked MacDuff's question of a number of bishops, and one cardinal, and received not very satisfactory replies. The impression remains that the religious view of life is that it's a kind of unpleasant obstacle race in which those who suffer man-made, or natural cruelties qualify for a post-mortem reward. The question that remains is what sort of a character would impose such miseries on a helpless humanity, and whether the setter of such terrible obstacles can truly claim to be all loving. In this respect the Greek gods, squabbling among themselves, deceitful, adulterous and given to fickle favouritism and irrational rage, seem far more likely to be in charge than any single, benevolent deity.

The best explanation for God's behaviour I received was of Malcolm Muggeridge. 'God', he said, 'is the supreme dramatist and the Shakespeare of the skies. You can't write a satisfactory play without villains, so real, live Lady Macbeths, Iagos and Gonerils have to be created.' All that can be said in answer to that is that the mortal playwright is only dealing with actors and, in his works, no one really dies.

If God's ultimate purposes seem to be of doubtful morality, I have no such reservations about the social and ethical message of the New Testament. I count myself a leading member of the Atheists for Christ Brigade, and I don't think it requires a faith in a personal God to believe in a society based on the precepts contained in the Sermon on the Mount. For me Christianity's great and unique contribution to the world lies in its affirmation of the supreme importance of the individual soul. The old religions of Greece and Rome, for all their wonderfully poetic truths, their understanding of fate and human fallibility, would never have led to the freeing of slaves and the social reforms of the last centuries. The religions of the East have never sufficiently recognized the independence and significance of the individual. So this apparent contradiction exists. The politics I have adopted, the just society I believe we should all work for, come from the Victorian Christian Socialists and the preachers in non-conformist chapels. The painting and the poetry I love, in which the importance of the individual's life is mixed with sunny memories of a pagan world, has, in the main, been produced by Christian artists and writers. We have been fortunate enough to inherit Christian faith as well as Roman stoicism in Shakespeare, and the Christian approach to beauty and the majesty of the world in the works of Piero della Francesca and Michelangelo. You must understand, and indeed love, Christianity to understand and love our literature, just as you must understand and have an affection for the Greek gods to enjoy the *Iliad* and the *Odyssey*.

So I feel, and feel grateful to be part of a Christian civilization, whether or not I can accept the existence of a personal deity. If this seems like getting the best of both worlds, doing so doesn't seem to me a bad way to live.

The other great defence of a belief in God is that, true or not, the idea of a celestial Lord Chief Justice, able to mete out dire punishments and eternal rewards, keeps us all behaving well. Why should we be kind, caring and compassionate, help the poor and remain honest unless there's something in it for us? This somewhat simplistic view of religion never worked. When a belief in hell was almost universal robbery, murder and blood stained tyranny flourished. Most of us refrain from mugging old ladies or raping young girls not because of the fear of prison, but because that's not the sort of behaviour we approve of in others or ourselves. It is probably true to say that the fear of punishment, whether of prison, death, or hell fire, has never done much to reduce the crime rate.

The Victorian agnostics, George Eliot among them, took the view that living without God meant that you had to behave better, with greater kindness, honesty and consideration for others, because you were doing it on your own responsibility and not on divine orders. The example of my own mother and father led me early to the conclusion that good behaviour doesn't depend of the hopes and fears of punishment and reward.

A belief in human justice, in progress towards a fairer society on earth, in fundamental decency rather than original sin, is, in itself, an act of faith; but not necessarily of religious faith. Religion plays little part in the works of Chekhov, sympathy with human weakness is almost all. Trofimov, the eternal student in *The Cherry Orchard*, speaks of hopes in what Noel Coward called 'life *before* death'. 'The earth is great and beautiful,' Trofimov says. 'There are many beautiful things in it.' And he already has a 'foreboding of happiness. I see glimpses of it already. Yes, the moon is rising. It is coming nearer and nearer; already I can hear its footsteps. Here is happiness – here it comes! And if we never see it – if we may never know it – what does it matter? Others will see it after us.'

It is this faith in a human future, only to be achieved, as Trofimov says, by hard and laborious work, that I find much more moving than hopes of heaven.

Living without God does not therefore mean living without faith. The most cogent criticism of such an attitude is that a godless life may mean nothing more than soulless materialism and the sort of aridness represented by the old anti-religious museums in the Soviet Union. A sense of awe and mystery is an essential element of the human condition, and how, if God departs, can this sense be gratified?

This is no doubt where the arts, in which awe, wonder and a sense of mystery are vital ingredients, are so important. With the decline of religion it is even more important that the arts, rather than science and mathematics, are seen as the basis of education. It's also essential to keep a continuing sense of wonder at the power and beauty of nature and Wordsworth's pantheism may be as near as we can get to religion without a personal deity.

> For I have learned
> To look on nature, not as in the hour
> Of thoughtless youth; but hearing oftentimes
> The still, sad music of humanity ...
> And I have felt
> A presence that disturbs me with the joy
> Of elevated thoughts; a sense sublime
> Of something far more deeply interfused,
> Whose dwelling is the light of setting suns,
> And the round ocean and the living air,
> And the blue sky, and in the mind of man.
>
> William Wordsworth
> *Tintern Abbey* (1798)